W9-DFO-481

# THE INDIAN POPULATION OF NEW ENGLAND
## IN THE SEVENTEENTH CENTURY

# The Indian Population
# of New England in the
# Seventeenth Century

By
S. F. COOK

UNIVERSITY OF CALIFORNIA PRESS

BERKELEY • LOS ANGELES • LONDON

University of California Publications in Anthropology


Volume 12
Approved for publication January 16, 1976




University of California Press
Berkeley and Los Angeles
California

University of California Press, Ltd.
London, England

ISBN 0-520-09553-7
Library of Congress Catalog Card No.: 76-3884

# CONTENTS

Prefatory Note
Chapter
    I. General Considerations    1
   II. New Hampshire and Northeastern Massachusetts:
       The Pennacook Confederacy    13
  III. Southeastern Massachusetts and the Islands    29
  IV. Rhode Island, Eastern Connecticut, Central and
       Western Massachusetts    46
   V. Western Connecticut and the Lower Hudson Valley:
       The Wappinger Confederacy    60
  VI. The Upper Hudson Valley and Long Island    75
Summary    84
Bibliography    85

# PREFATORY NOTE

Although he had chosen to spend most of his adult life on the coast of the Pacific Ocean, Sherburne Cook never forgot the region of his birth and early manhood, New England. (He was born and reared in Springfield, Massachusetts.) In the last years of his life, he decided to return, for part of his studies, to the Indians of his native region, and published a number of short papers on them. When he died on 7 November 1974, he left a manuscript on the aboriginal population of New England at the time of the coming of the Europeans. It was a theme he had pursued brilliantly for other regions, most notably for California and Mexico.

The manuscript was complete except for a title, a map, minor editorial clarifications, and the verifications of citations and bibliography that any typescript is likely to require. Accordingly, rather than indicate each change or addition by the cumbersome use of brackets, we explain here the general nature of the editing and additions.

In accordance with the wishes of Sherburne Cook, and of his family after his death, I have served as literary executor. I have been greatly helped by Robert Heizer of the Department of Anthropology, Berkeley, a long-time friend and co-author of Cook. The manuscript was edited by Mrs. Grace Buzaljko, whose services were kindly made available by the Department of Anthropology of the Berkeley campus. Mrs. Adrienne Morgan, who prepared so many maps and graphs for Cook in the past, has drawn the map. The additional research for clarification of citations was done by Eric Van Young of the Department of History, as research assistant.

Funds for the research and the preparation of clean typescript came from the Committee on Research of the Berkeley campus, which over the years showed a generous understanding of studies not easily fitted within any departmental frame. The often voiced verbal appreciation of Sherburne Cook for the work of the Committee should again be put into print. Finally, mention should be made of the generosity of the Cook family, whose only desire has been to make the study available to the scholarly public, and of the kindness of the departments of History and Anthropology in helping to carry out that desire.

Woodrow Borah

Chapter 1

# GENERAL CONSIDERATIONS

The Indian population which is discussed here coincides only approximately with the present-day boundaries of New England. To the northeast we establish a line along the western border of Maine so as to exclude the Abnaki. This important tribe is cut off from the Indians of the rest of New England primarily because of its environment and the fact that the Maine Indians differed in many respects, ecological and political, from those to the south. Hence we begin with the Pennacook, who held the basin of the Merrimac north to Lakes Winnepesaukee and Ossipee, and who extended westward to the Connecticut and eastward to the Saco River in Maine.

The Massachusetts and Rhode Island tribes are familiar to all historians, as are those of the Connecticut Valley upstream as far as the southern borders of Vermont and New Hampshire. The Connecticut Valley beyond this point was undoubtedly inhabited, but concerning it and almost the entire state of Vermont we have relatively little information. Certainly between the Connecticut River and the Iroquois in New York there were few, if any, permanent Indian settlements, although the intervening Green Mountain region must have been used by both Algonkian and Iroquois hunting and raiding parties. Some students have wished to extend this expanse of empty territory southward through the Berkshires of Massachusetts well into the state of Connecticut.

Central and southern Massachusetts and Connecticut had relatively intense Indian occupancy as did Rhode Island. Southwestern Connecticut and Long Island were densely populated. The Wappinger Confederacy covered both southeastern New York and southwestern Connecticut. It is therefore preferable to extend the limits of the New England province so as to include all the land east of the Hudson River and south of Albany. The Hudson forms a more natural line of demarcation than the state boundaries and does less violence to the aboriginal distribution of Indian tribes. James Mooney (1928: p. 4), in his division called the "North Atlantic States," used much the same segregation of territory, except that he included the Iroquois of New York, the Munsee, Delaware, and the Conestoga of New Jersey and Pennsylvania. For the region which is considered here he shows a total aboriginal population of 34,100. For the five New England states alone he allows 22,100, with 12,000 on Long Island and in mainland New York east of the Hudson and south of Albany.

In assessing the magnitude of an aboriginal population we depend initially upon direct statements or estimates made by contemporary or modern authorities. If these apply to only a fraction of the total population being considered, they may with care be extrapolated to the whole. In addition, certain constants, or indices, based upon correlated entities are of great value, provided that they can be determined with reasonable fidelity.

1

# KEY TO MAP

## MAJOR TRIBES, SUBTRIBES, AND CENTERS OF POPULATION ABOUT 1630

### PENNACOOK CONFEDERACY

1. Pennacook proper
2. Winnepesaukee
3. Coosuc
4. Ossipee
5. Pequaket
6. Newichawanoc
7. Accominta
8. Piscatequa
9. Souhegan
10. Nashua
11. Wachusett
12. Wamesit
13. Pentucket
14. Squamscot
15. Winnecowet
16. Agawam
17. Naumkeag

### NARRAGANSETT

1. Shawomet
2. Narragansett

### WAPPINGER CONFEDERACY

1. Tunxis
2. Poquonnoc — Massoco — Sicaog
3. Podunk
4. Mattabesec proper
5. Wongunk
6. Hammonasset
7. Menunketuck
8. Quinnipiack
9. Paugusset
10. Uncowa
11. Tankiteke
12. Siwanoy
13. Sint-sink — Kitchawanc
14. Nochpeem — Wappinger proper
15. Weckquaesgeek
16. Manhattan

### LONG ISLAND

1. Canarsee Montauk

### NIPMUCK — POCUMTUC

1. Nipmuck proper
2. Wabaquasset
3. Quinnebaug
4. Quaboag
5. Pocumtuc proper
6. Agawam
7. Shipmuck
8. Nonotuck — Norwottuc — Waranoke
9. Squawkeag

### MASSACHUSETT

### WAMPANOAG

### NAUSET

### MOHEGAN — PEQUOT

### MAHICAN

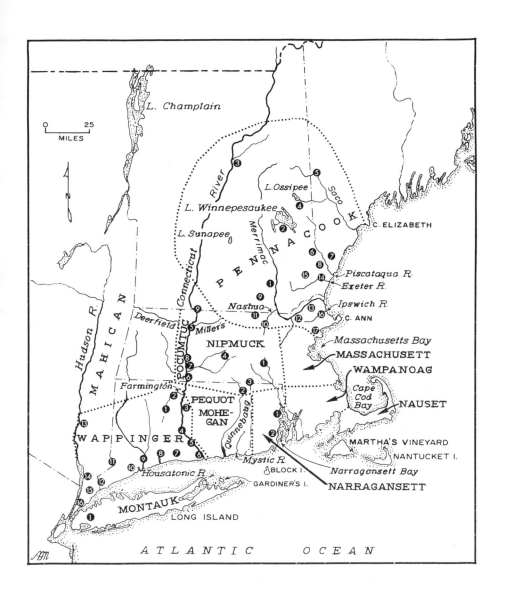

One such parameter is family size, with which may be included the proportion of able-bodied men (warriors) in the population. A second is the number of those who dwelled in a house, for the number of houses is often recorded. The third entity is the village or settlement, with regard to which the size in area or in population may be known. Moreover, the number of such settlements often affords a valuable clue. In the analysis of these factors we may depend for information upon the written evidence left by observers, or upon the later findings of archaeologists. Finally, it is sometimes feasible to utilize the volume of specific items of subsistence which were grown, gathered, or caught by the people.

For every cultural province in the ancient or aboriginal world, it is necessary to compute these indices anew, because no single society repeats with identity the quantitative features of another. Even within a selected region minor distinctions can be made. Whether they should be recognized depends upon their magnitude relative to the precision which may be desired in the estimate for the entire province. For instance, in New England the family size and the proportion of fighting men in the population probably varied little from that found in the West and South, whereas the village size (and population) may have been very different from that of other areas. Some discussion of each parameter is therefore necessary with respect to that portion of New England and eastern New York which we have outlined as the locus of investigation.

### ESTIMATES OF FAMILY SIZE

Among primitive peoples the biological family usually consists of a procreating couple together with their children. The latter averages two or three depending on the demographic status of the population. Frequently, because of death or desertion, only one spouse is present, with the living children. The social family, on the other hand, includes one or more relatives, such as a brother, grandfather, aunt, and the like. If, then, we assume a condition of normal maintenance equilibrium, the biological family should reach a minimum average of four persons, and the social family an average of five, or perhaps six. Under favorable conditions and with an increasing population, the biological family should demonstrate a mean of five persons, and the social family six to seven. It may be expected that the family number in an undisturbed society would ordinarily attain a mean of six.

For New England, I know of no estimates which were made of family size as it existed before the incoming Europeans had badly upset the natural equilibrium in the native population. Indeed, the only data at hand relate to the villages of "praying Indians," or native residues which persisted into the eighteenth century. Among these people living conditions were very poor, the total population was dwindling and the observed family number could scarcely have represented the normal condition.

In 1674, Daniel Gookin (p. 205 n.), the noted Indian missionary, wrote that on Martha's Vineyard there were six villages, with 155 families and 800 souls. This is equivalent to 5.17 persons per family. He also computed the population of several other places by using a factor of 5 per family. In 1761, the Rev. John Devotion reported for the Montauks of Long Island 33 families with 162 souls, or 4.91 persons per family. Holmes (1804: p. 76) said that the residue of the Mohegans in 1799 had a total of 84 persons in 25 families, or 3.36 persons per family. This was, to be sure, a moribund, almost defunct group. At the other extreme is a report on the Groton Reservation in Connecticut in 1762 (Anonymous, 1809). There were 15 families with 30 adults and 92 children, 8 widows with 8 children, 3 single men, and 1 single woman. The 15 families by themselves averaged 8.13 persons; if the 8 widows with children are counted as families the average was exactly six persons.

It will be noted that Gookin used a factor of five in his estimates. The cases cited above come to nearly the same value. In the eighteenth century, therefore, five persons seems to have been the mean number in each family. However, by this time the Indian population was deteriorating very rapidly, even in those units which were more or less protected. In the aboriginal condition the number must have been greater, for at that period the Indians were maintaining their population, if not increasing it. A minimum average array of numbers for each family must have included two parents, two children, and two relatives, a total of six. In a healthy society more than two children would be expected, and the total should have reached closer to seven than to six. However, a value of six may be assumed as a reasonable average for the social family in the aboriginal condition.

A closely allied magnitude is the proportion of active males in the total population. This fraction was usually expressed as the collective body of fighting men, or warriors. The number was relatively stable, because in the Indian social system every male between the approximate ages of 15 and 50 took part in military operations, or at least could be counted on for this service if extreme need arose. It is possible, therefore, to utilize data from a very wide area, indeed from almost all of North America. Under pre-white conditions, and in normal times, the proportion of males between the ages mentioned would fluctuate within a narrow range around a constant value. Since the number of all Indians was most frequently expressed by Europeans in terms of fighting units, this proportion becomes of great significance for the estimate of population.

The Polish demographer Krzywicki (1934: pp. 322-541) devoted much attention to this problem. In his Appendices II and III, in which he lists nearly every Indian tribe north of Mexico, he cites all sources known to him which give estimates of population and also of the number of warriors. A detailed examination of these appendices yields a total of 258 cases in which there is a figure for both population and warriors from the same tribe. The mean value is 4.104 for the ratio of general population to each warrior. The standard deviation is 1.355, and the standard error is 0.084. Krzywicki also cites (*ibid.*: p. 318, n. 1) a work by H. M. Brackenridge (1814), who assembled data directly. He says:

H. M. Brackenridge 1811, estimated this ratio for forty-six tribes: in twenty-one of these, the ratio varied between 1:3 and 1:4; in twelve cases it was between 1:4 and 1:5; the remaining tribes split up into two equal groups, one above and one below the norms just quoted.

We may take the half-way points, 3.5 for the 21 tribes, 4.5 for the 12 tribes. Then we may use 2.5 and 5.5 each for half the remaining 13 tribes. The average is then

4.0 general population to warriors. There is no way to evaluate the quality of Brackenridge's estimates, but the closeness of his average, as calculated in the manner indicated, to that of Krzywicki is striking. In view of the lack of any evidence to the contrary, we may use 4.0 as an approximation to the ratio of population to warriors. Likewise, since no evidence exists to indicate otherwise, we may consider that the New England Indians resembled those of the continent at large, and that the ratio in this area was also 4.0.

### ESTIMATES OF OCCUPANTS PER HOUSE

The structure of houses, together with their furnishings and the domestic pattern which revolved around them, has been the subject of innumerable essays ever since the first Europeans landed on North American shores. On all parts of the continent the domestic economy of the natives delighted and interested observant white men and volumes were written concerning all phases of Indian daily life. Here we need be concerned with only one small aspect of the entire field: how many people lived in a house. There are frequent references to the numbers of dwelling units and, if we knew the average capacity of these, it would not be difficult to estimate the population.

In New England, as in most of North America, there were two types of houses, one large and multifamily, the other small and single-family. The small house was the more common and the more temporary, for it could be easily moved according to season or to economic and military pressure. This is the familiar wigwam of American folklore, the term most frequently applied by all commentators on Indian life in New England. The large, multifamily shelter was the longhouse. The distinction between the two types appears not to have been absolute, for some of the wigwams came to approach in floor space the smaller representatives of the larger, communal type. Nevertheless, when the term wigwam is used, the smaller, single-family dwelling is customarily meant.

Some notion of the usual number of occupants of ordinary Indian houses throughout the United States and Canada can be obtained by an analysis of Krzywicki's appendices (1934: pp. 322-541), previously mentioned. In many instances he has cited statements from observers or historians which give both the number of houses and number of inhabitants for certain tribes and villages. It is possible to segregate these according to a broad geographical classification and for each region to derive the average number of persons per house. Five areas show the following figures:

|   | Number of Cases | Mean Number of Persons Per House |
|---|---|---|
| 1. Columbia River Province | 35 | 32.66 |
| 2. Southwest and Great Basin | 8 | 6.63 |
| 3. Plains | 75 | 9.18 |
| 4. South coast | 17 | 8.49 |
| 5. Eastern forest and north | 16 | 8.56 |

New England would fall in group 5, the mean for which differs by an insignificant amount from those of groups 3 and 4. The southwestern houses contained slightly fewer people, and the Columbia River tribes — mostly according to the reports of Lewis and Clark — lived almost exclusively in multifamily homes. The average for groups 3, 4, and 5, collectively, is very close to 9 persons per house. Some multifamily, or transitional, dwellings may be included here. Hence for New England the mean may be reduced to 8 as a working value.

In this connection a passage from Purchas' *Pilgrimage* is of interest. Thornton (1857: p. 155) discusses a section from Purchas (*Pilgrimage,* London edition, 1673-1674: Vol. 4, p. 155) in which occurs a description of a semilegendary country called Mawooshen, which stretched along the coast of Maine. Many rivers and towns were mentioned, most of which cannot be identified. However, among others, three villages are named: Penobscot, with 50 houses and 80 men; Chabegnadose, with 30 houses and 90 men; and Meecomb, with 50 houses and 80 men. The total of the three is 130 houses and 250 men, or 1.92 men per house. The geography may be largely fictional, but the allocation of houses and men to the villages would seem to be founded upon fact. Such explicit numbers would hardly be given unless they approached the truth. Since the houses on the average contained nearly two men, they must have been occupied by either two families or a single extended family. In any event, if we apply the factor of four as the proportion of general population to men, we get a mean of 7.68 persons per house, a figure not far from 8.0 as derived from the data of Krzywicki.

Other descriptions of New England dwellings are conflicting with respect to size and floor space. The small, single-family wigwam and the multifamily longhouse appear to predominate, with the former in the decided majority. The construction of the wigwam was variable, but the size, and hence the capacity for living quarters, was relatively uniform. We have a few specific figures. Williamson (1839: Vol. 1, p. 489), after describing multifamily houses, says that ordinary wigwams were conical, 12 to 15 feet in diameter. Roger Williams in the *Key* (1643: p. 48) says: "The families will live completely and lovingly in a little round house of some fourteen or sixteen feet over. . . ." Here the range of diameter is approximately 12 to 16 feet.

According to data on California studied by the present author (Cook and Heizer; 1968: pp. 90-91) many groups of houses there which contained six persons fell in this size range. Indeed, it was calculated that the minimum possible floor space which could support one person was 20 square feet. If this value is applied to the New England houses, the wigwams could have held 5 to 10 persons, depending upon the exact size.

ESTIMATES OF VILLAGE SIZE

Further information may be derived from the size of settlements and the number and arrangement of houses. That these were closely packed is indicated by several comments. For instance, Ellis and Morris (1906: p. 11) note that in general, "the wigwams were pitched closely together and the village seldom occupied more than from three to four acres." With respect to the Pequot fort on the Mystic River in Connecticut, Vincent (1638) wrote that "this fort was so crowded with these numerous dwellings that the English wanted foot room to grapple with their adversaries." He also noted that the area consisted of "at least two acres of ground."

The Pequot fort on the Mystic makes an interesting test case. Vincent says that the total area was two acres. Benjamin Trumbull (1767: p. 23) notes that it contained about 70 wigwams. Two acres is equivalent to 87,000 square feet. If there were 70 wigwams, each preempted an area of 1,243 square feet, roughly a 35-foot square. If the average diameter of the wigwams was 17.5 feet, then they were spaced on the average one diameter apart. This is very close and could well restrict the "foot room" of the English. A diameter of 17.5 feet gives a floor area of almost 250 square feet. The absolute maximum number of persons who could be accommodated in such space would be 12; a much more reasonable figure is 8 or 10. It is interesting that Trumbull (1767: p. 23) says that the fort held 400 to 500 persons. Seventy wigwams with 450 persons would have meant 6.4 persons per wigwam.

Another estimate of settlement area is given by Sylvester (1910: Vol. 2, p. 260) for King Philip's village at Pocasset. Here were "above a hundred wigwams . . . covering about 4 acres of ground." It may be assumed that in a permanent village, rather than a fort constructed for an emergency, the dwellings would be more widely spaced. At the fort there were 35 wigwams per acre; here there were 25 or more. The individual size may be taken as substantially the same.

A further instructive case is that of the Wappinger village of Weckquaesgeek, as described by Bolton (1881: Vol. 1, pp. 8-9). The dwellings, called huts by Bolton, were arranged in three streets, each 80 paces long. A pace is about 3 feet. Thus the total length of the three streets was about 720 feet. The huts may be assumed to have been placed on both sides of each street. Then the total foot frontage was 720 x 2, or 1,440 feet. Each hut must have required at least 24 front feet, and if so, there would have been a minimum of 60 huts. We do not know the precise shape of the hut or its depth, but the intervening space between huts must have equalled the distance across one hut. This distance would then have been approximately 12 feet. If the house were conical there would have been slightly more than 100 square feet of floor space. If the shape were rectangular the area could have been greater and could have accommodated a single extended family. We have no direct estimate of population, although it was claimed that 500 or more Indians perished in the massacre which took place at this village in 1643. However, just before the massacre the town had been the scene of an Indian festival, and no one knows how many visitors there were from other villages.

The large, multifamily house was much more conspicuous and impressive than the lowly wigwam, and consequently has received considerable attention. Daniel Gookin (1674: p. 150) describes these structures as being of several sizes, usually from 20 to 40 feet long, although he had seen some 60 to 100 feet long and 30 feet broad. "In the greater houses they make two, three or four fires." A fire represented a family, albeit an extended one. Williamson (1839: Vol. 1, p. 489) distinguishes between the "ordinary" wigwams and the "best" wigwams, which were 20 to 40 feet long and in width were roughly 2/3 of the long dimension. These "frequently" contained four families to a dwelling. Ruttenber (1872: p. 75) describes the houses of the Wappinger. They rarely exceeded 20 feet in width and "were sometimes a hundred and eighty yards long." Hodge (*Handbook,* 1907: Part I, p. 788) more correctly says 180 feet long. Ruttenber (1872: p. 75) claims that from 16 to 18 families might have occupied one house, according to its size. This is an incredible statement, for it would imply over 100 people. An excellent discussion of the New England houses is that of Bushnell (1919: pp. 18-29), who gives further examples.

Without citing further references, we may consider that the communal house ranged in size from 10 to 20 feet in width and 20 to 100 feet in length. The extreme cases beyond these limits must have been very few, or else the edifices must have been used for purposes other than ordinary living. The normal area, therefore, would have run from 200 to 2,000 square feet. The customary estimate of number of families per communal house is from 2 to 4. The limits may be extended to cover other, probable cases to a range of 1 to 5 families. Then the floor space per family would have been in the range of 200 to 400 square feet. The total area would have accommodated extended families of 8 to 12 persons, or a total of 8 to 60 occupants per structure.

This crude calculation shows that on the whole it is very difficult to arrive at a firm *average* value for either the size or the capacity of the communal house. The result is that we must forego, as impracticable, the use of any universal relationship between the number of communal houses and the total number of occupants. On the contrary, it is necessary, if the pertinent information exists in the written documents, to make individual estimates for each tribe or community. At the same time the capacity of the small, single-family dwelling may be regarded as 8 persons.

Villages or other settlements may be considered with respect to size, or number of inhabitants, and to their frequency and distribution. For the New England area there is no fixed rule for size. The range is from very small — two or three families — at one extreme to several hundred persons at the other. We are therefore forced in individual cases to depend upon the statements, which are often couched in terms of warriors, or houses, are likely to be somewhere near correct, for the numbers involved are nearly always within the limits of human observation, and there was little motivation for exaggeration or deliberate falsehood. On the other hand, writers of all types naturally have been prone to emphasize the larger and more important places. Here are a few samples.

*Bolton* (1881: Vol. 1, pp. 8-9), cited above, states that a castle of the Weckquaesgeek in 1663 had 80 warriors. If this number is multiplied by 4, the village had 320 persons.

*Drake* (1851: p. 116) says that at the time of the invasion of 1636, Block Island had two plantations with 60 wigwams. At 8 persons per wigwam this means 240 persons per plantation.

*Gookin* (1674: p. 188) lists 14 villages of praying Indians. The average size was

79 persons, but this was a moribund population. An editorial note added to
the 1792 publication states that in 1720 on Martha's Vineyard there were
six "small" villages, the average size of which was 133 persons per village.

*Governor Thomas Hinckley* (1685: p. 133) listed 16 groups of Indian survivors
in the Colony of New Plymouth. The average number per group was 90
persons.

*Hubbard* (1680: pp. 31-34), speaking of villages, says: "At every one of these
places there used to be, if commodious, about an hundred or two hundred
inhabitants."

*Strachey* (1612: pp. 231, 243), reporting on Popham's expedition of 1607, says
that at River Pemaquid they found an Indian Village of "a hundred men,
women, and children." On the Kennebec below Waterville there was a village
with "neere fifty able men"; for the Kennebec village we can estimate about
200 people.

*Sylvester* (1910: Vol. 2, p. 260) mentions that Philip's village at Pocasset Swamp
in 1675 contained above a hundred wigwams. At 8 persons each, this is a
total of 800 persons.

*Thornton* (1857: p. 155), quoting Purchas, mentions three Maine villages, two
with 80 and one with 90 men. (These villages have already been discussed
above with respect to houses.) At 4 persons per "man," there were two
villages with 320, and one with 360 inhabitants.

*Ellis and Morris* (1906) assembled cases of Indian villages destroyed during King
Philip's War. For example: Menamesit (p. 95): 50 wigwams, or an estimated
400 people.
Pumham's village (p. 158): 100 wigwams, or 800 people. Village of the Squaw
sachem (p. 145): 150 wigwams, or 1,200 people.

These citations, and many others which could be adduced, give the impression
that Indian villages encountered by the English, which were large enough to warrant
mention, ranged from about 100 to 250 persons. Abnormal conditions such as war
or disease could either increase or decrease the number, but only in the fortified
towns of the Wappinger and allied tribes did the aboriginal normal level rise much
above 250 to 300 inhabitants. Of smaller places which left no trace we can say
little, save that they must have added significantly to the total population. Estimates of size must depend upon evaluation of the evidence available in each instance.

In the absence of specific testimony it is very difficult to determine the aggregate
number of settlements within any particular territory, tribal or regional. The
obstacle to a true count is primarily, in New England at least, the temporary character of the villages. Many authors have described the almost universal tendency of
the Indians to move their domicile, often to fit the seasons or the type of food
supply, but often for no ascertainable reason. The traces of habitation left at a
certain locality often give little indication of the time during which the spot was
occupied. Thus, from the famous description in Mourt's *Relation* (1622: p. 235)
of the Taunton River: "As we passed along we observed that there were few places

by the river but had been inhabited" no concrete number can be assigned to the settlements which previously had existed there simultaneously.

Particularly does impermanence of habitation become a strong negative factor in the attempt to determine population when the evidence is not historical but archaeological. Here the time element is especially important, for if the occupancy of a site was only brief and the entire span of years in which a group occupied an area was long, the total number of sites may be vastly greater than the number of those occupied simultaneously. Unless we know, or can make a wise guess at the relative fraction of simultaneously occupied sites, we are helpless.

However, in making this guess, and in spite of the difficulties just pointed out, certain clues may aid us in ascertaining the number of settlements. The first is the character of the individual sites themselves. A site may be clearly a habitation area, with domestic remains, such as animal bones and charcoal, as well as residues of houses. It may be a camp site or a slaughter site, where game was dressed. It may be a shell midden on the shore, where the natives came seasonally to gather clams and oysters. The latter are obviously temporary settlements. The habitation site, although occupied intermittently throughout the year, was permanent in the sense that the people consistently returned to it and used it as a base of operations.

A second clue for the archaeologist is the quantity of debris which has been left. A thick deposit of kitchen midden, for example, surely denotes a relatively long period of occupancy, even if intermittent. Conversely, a few stone implements or weapons scattered over a large area indicate that the occupation was very brief and probably for some purpose associated with the securing of food. A shell midden, unaccompanied by true habitation residues, implies only a seasonal occupation of a few days or weeks.

A third clue lies in the identification of kind and number of artifacts. If they are present in great quantity, and if they are both utilitarian and ornamental, the site may be regarded as permanent. Not only the number and kind, but the probable date as determined stratigraphically or typologically, is important, for the presence only of artifacts long antedating the era of colonization denies the active occupation of the site just before the European invasion. At the other extreme, the presence of metalware or porcelain identifies the locality as one used after the arrival of the white man.

These simple rules are not only helpful but essential to the use of village or settlement number as a basis for calculating precontact population. However, few cases exist where purely archaeological data are decisive in establishing a final value. This source of evidence must be combined, where possible, with information derived from the written word.

### ESTIMATES FROM SUBSISTENCE LEVELS

A quite different approach to the estimate of population has been pursued by numerous investigators of prehistory in many parts of the world. They have attempted to analyze quantitatively the food resources of a region and then to compute the population which could be supported by the amount of subsistence available. This method has been relatively successful in areas where the quantity of food consumed can be determined within reasonable limits. Such regions are likely to be those in which the inhabitants subsisted on a single staple crop, such as corn or manioc in the western world, or in which the total intake from several sources can be estimated and assessed dietetically. These prerequisites are not met in New England.

We know from a multiplicity of accounts and descriptions that the New England Indians utilized several types of subsistence. They secured game by hunting, princi- pally in the winter; they gathered great quantities of shellfish, as is attested by the extensive middens which are still to be seen on the coast; they were very successful fishermen in both lakes and rivers; they utilized wild plant food, such as roots and berries; they planted and harvested a great deal of corn, particularly in the milder climate of southern New England. Of all these sources, the only one for which the data might support a quantitative calculation of nutritional value is corn. The extent to which modern scholarship has carried the analysis of corn culture can be judged from the papers by Delabarre and Wilder (1920), Butler (1948), and Laurent (1959). Some of this work is very interesting and indicates a trend which may in the future lead to a fundamental evaluation of the entire dietary status, as well as the probable population of not only New England but of the entire northeastern United States and Canada. An excellent beginning has been made by Bennett (1955) in his essay on the food economy of the New England Indians. At the present juncture, however, we can employ subsistence levels only sparingly and occasionally.

The following chapters examine the evidence for, and arrive at, new estimates of the Indian population at various times during the seventeenth century. The aim is a better estimate of numbers at or just before substantial contact with the Europeans (i.e., the beginning of the seventeenth century). The area is New England without Maine but with Long Island and the eastern Hudson Valley for the reasons already given. For discussion I divide this area into regions, each region being the subject of one chapter: the Pennacook Confederacy in the northernmost region adjacent to Maine; southeastern Massachusetts and its islands; Rhode Island, eastern Connecticut, and central and western Massachusetts — a diverse region with sub- regions; the Wappinger Confederacy in western Connecticut and the lower Hudson Valley; and finally the Mahican in the upper Hudson Valley and Long Island. A brief summary brings together my estimates for a total figure for the entire region.

Chapter 2

# NEW HAMPSHIRE AND NORTHEASTERN MASSACHUSETTS: THE PENNACOOK CONFEDERACY

The Pennacook Confederacy occupied New Hampshire, northeastern Massachusetts, and the southern tip of Maine. The Confederacy was mentioned by Gookin, who wrote in 1674. The passage occurs in his *Historical Collections,* published in 1792 (pp. 148-149), where he described the Pawtucket, later identified with the Wamesit. These people, he said, were over the Pennacook, Agawam, and several other tribes, and altogether they contained "about three thousand men," that is, warriors. At the ratio of four to one, 3,000 warriors implies a total population of 12,000 souls. This figure has been in doubt ever since Gookin suggested it. It was quoted by Hoyt (1824: p. 88), by Drake (1867: pp. 8-9), and by Day (1962: p. 29) without adverse criticism, but Krzywicki (1934: p. 518) and others have felt that 3,000 persons might have been meant rather than 3,000 men. However, even though the number may be an overestimate, there is no reason to suppose that Gookin meant less than he said.

James Mooney and Cyrus Thomas, who wrote the short article on the Pennacook in the *Handbook of American Indians* (Hodge, 1910: Part II, pp. 225-226) say that by 1630 the number had been reduced to 2,500, and by 1674 to 1,250. The phrase "had been reduced" implies an earlier much greater number. Mooney and Thomas give no references for their statements, but clearly the 1630 estimate is derived from Governor Thomas Dudley's letter (1631) in Force's *Tracts* (1838: p. 6). Dudley said that the chief Passaconaway had 400-500 men. If the multiplicative factor is raised to five, the population might have been 2,500. Mooney and Thomas's figure probably comes from Gookin (1792), who wrote that the tribe in 1674 contained not above 250 men, besides women and children. After King Philip's War many of the Pennacook were tricked into surrender to the notorious Major Waldron at Dover, New Hampshire, and sold as slaves. Others migrated to the Hudson Valley and to Quebec. Very few were left in their old habitat.

The decline from the aboriginal population must have been severe. It seems to have been precipitated by two factors, warfare and epidemics. The former involved principally the Mohawks. This easternmost division of the Iroquois raided the Pennacook tribes along the Merrimac and in northern Massachusetts with unusual intensity. A circumstantial account is given by Hadley (1903), who describes their assault on the tribal center at Concord, New Hampshire, with its three forts built specifically for defense against the Mohawk. Hadley thinks the effect of the attack has been exaggerated, but he says (p. 67): "The day may have been one of serious disaster; and may help to account for the weakened condition of the Pennacooks in 1623, as well as to suggest the date of the battle as being toward the end of the sixteenth century or early in the seventeenth." Percy S. Brown (1952) quotes ac-

13

counts stating that the Pennacook "before their destruction by the Mohawks" sometimes mustered 300 canoes at a single gathering.

Whether the Mohawk actually killed many people may be doubted, but there can be no question that they seriously disrupted the local economy and predisposed the survivors to epidemics. There are probably at least two of these which were lethal; plague and smallpox. The great plague of 1617 destroyed hundreds of Indians all along the coast from the Saco River south to Cape Cod. Ballard (1866: p. 429), in commenting upon the population decline in the vicinity of Concord, refers to the devastation caused by the Mohawk and continues: "It is possible, too, that the ravaging disease which swept off large numbers of natives on the sea coast . . . brought a portion of its desolation to this region." He mentions the frequent visits between the coastal people and those of the interior — visits which could easily have communicated the plague. Hadley (1903: p. 66) also remarks: "At their first historical appearance, about 1621, they [the Pennacook] had been much weakened by war, and other causes — among which may have been the dread disease of 1616, which prevailed along the sea-shore and at an unknown distance inland." Mooney and Thomas in the *Handbook* (Hodge, 1910: Part II, p. 225) ascribe the reduction in population to the smallpox, but, although there is plenty of evidence for its presence later than 1630, there is no direct reference to the disease prior to the arrival of the white man. After 1630, to be sure, it devastated the Indian population throughout the northeast and can hardly have spared the Pennacook.

In sum, the evidence indicates that the Pennacook Confederacy, or at least major parts of it, was in bad condition and suffering a serious depletion in population in the early years of white occupation. Hence, if there were approximately 2,500 persons in 1630, there may have been many times that number a few years previously. It will be advantageous, now, to turn to the component fractions of the entire group.

The Pennacook were clearly an aggregation of smaller units, some of which had little more than village status. The constituent parts are presented in different lists by different writers, and in such a manner as to create rather than resolve confusion. Hubbard (1680) was one of the first to attempt to specify groups. In his *General History* (pp. 31-34) he lists twenty "societies" which inhabited New England. Of these, no. 4 was the Piscatequa and no. 5 was the Merrimac to 50 miles above the mouth of the river. Along the lower Merrimac were found the Wamesit, Pentucket, Patucket, Amoskeag, Pennacook, and others. No. 6 included the people near the mouth of the river at Newbury, Massachusetts; and no. 7 the Agawam at Ipswich and the Naumkeag at Salem, Massachusetts. Kidder (1859: p. 236) said that the Pennacook were the only inhabitants of the Merrimac basin and "perhaps included nearly all the nations who resided in what is now the state of New Hampshire." He mentions as branches of the Pennacook the Pennatucket, Wambesite, Souhegan, all of the Indians on the Piscataqua River, plus the Cowasack on the upper Connecticut. Barstow (1842: p. 22) mentions a tribe at Exeter; one at Dover; the Pascatequa, the Ossipee, the Pennacook on the Merrimac, and the Coos Indians to the headwaters of the Connecticut. All these were confederated under Passaconaway.

Farmer (1824: p. 219) says that the Pennacook inhabited the Merrimac River "many miles" above and below Concord. Under Passaconaway were the Agawam, Naumkeag, Pascatequa, Accominta, and others. Sylvester (1910: Vol. 2, p. 41) copied a list of Hoyt (1824: p. 89), who called the entire group Pawtucket, and mentioned the Pennacook, Agawam, Naumkeag, Piscataway, Accominta, and Newichawannock. The Pennacook included the Wambesit, Souhegan, and Cowasack.

The most authoritative modern formulation is that by Mooney and Thomas in the *Handbook* (Hodge, 1910: Part II, pp. 225-226). They say that the tribes directly composing the confederacy were the Agawam, Wamesit, and Nashua in Massachusetts, and the Souhegan, Amoskeag, Pennacook, and Winnepesaukee in New Hampshire. They also included the Accominta of Maine and the Naumkeag of Massachusetts (Essex County), together with the Wachusett, Coosuc, Squamscot, Winnecowet, Piscatequa, and Newichawanoc. In their list of "Pennacook villages and bands" they exclude Naumkeag, but include Pentucket, Wamesit, Ossipee, and Washacum. In view of the many contradictions and uncertainties surrounding the status and existence of these small tribelets, it will be advisable to consider them separately in order to ascertain what is known of their probable population. More-over, it is easier to make estimates of numbers if the political units are more or less precisely defined. We use the *Handbook* classification as a basis and consider 17 tribelets or villages.

### THE PENNACOOK PROPER

This tribe is placed by most writers at Concord, New Hampshire (Farmer, 1824: p. 219; Williamson, 1839: Vol. 1, p. 458; Barstow, 1842: p. 22; Ballard, 1866: p. 429; Hadley, 1903: p. 22; and Hodge, 1910: Part II, p. 226). The principal village is also stated to have been at Amoskeag Falls, which, according to Williamson, is at Concord. But Amoskeag Falls is downstream at Manchester, not at Concord, and there is a strong tradition that the villages at Amoskeag were visited at certain times of the year by Passaconaway in the early seventeenth century. Quite evidently both points were the focus of active Indian habitation. It is roughly 15 air miles from Manchester to Concord. Farmer (1824: p. 219) states that the Pennacook lived "many miles" above and below Concord on the Merrimac (say five miles). According to Marshall (1942), occupation sites were found at least five miles below Manchester. There was therefore a stretch of river perhaps 25 miles long which was thickly inhabited.

The map drawn by Marshall shows seven sites (perhaps six) on the Merrimac below Manchester, of which two were villages; the others were camp grounds or cemeteries. One of the villages was a quarter-mile long. The other covered 100 acres. Both seem to have been permanently occupied in late precolonial times. On a small affluent to the Merrimac, and at Massabesic Lake, five miles to the east, there were two other village sites, the second a "large settlement." From the sizes mentioned, and from the number of artifacts found (10,000 collected from a single site), it may be surmised that there was a normal average of 200 inhabitants in each village. The Manchester area, therefore, may have contained 800 persons.

Since most historians have considered Concord as the center of Pennacook population, the Concord area must have comprehended more people than the Manchester
region. Perhaps, if we include the intervening river and the stretch above Concord
to the vicinity of Franklin, we might suppose another 1,200. The sum would then
be 2,000 for a distance of 35 miles on the Merrimac.

Another bit of archaeological evidence comes from the survey reported by
Moorehead (1931). The entire Merrimac River was explored and the principal
habitation sites were recorded. Moorehead noted 14 village sites on his map between Manchester and Webster Lake, near Franklin. To these may be added at
least two in the vicinity of Manchester which were described by Marshall, but
not mentioned by Moorehead. The total would be 16 for the Pennacook area.
Since Moorehead's village sites in distribution and size conform to the descriptions
given by earlier observers, they may be regarded as having been occupied during
the very late aboriginal period. An average of 200 inhabitants has been suggested
above, with some villages having perhaps 300, some only 100. This figure and
range is also supported by the reports cited previously concerning New England
villages in general. The final result is 3,200 people.

I am not aware of any contemporary observer who made an estimate of the
number of the Pennacook proper. Gookin's figure of 3,000 "men" applies to the
entire confederacy, as does probably Dudley's statement that Passaconaway controlled 400 or 500 warriors. Williamson (1839: p. 458) speaks of a tribe above the
Amoskeag Falls which had 3,000 "souls." He may well have been alluding to the
Pennacook. Potter (in Schoolcraft, 1865: Vol. 5, p. 230) gives two rather ambigu-
ous estimates. He starts with Dudley's statement that Passaconaway had under
his command "four or five hundred men," and then multiplies by a factor of three.
The result is "twelve to fifteen hundred souls." However, he then says, "Two
thousand would doubtless be a fair estimate for the tribe." It may be assumed
that the latter figure represents his final verdict.

Recently Brown (1952), referring to the river people, says, as has been mentioned previously, that they could muster 300 canoes. Since a minimum of two
able-bodied men was required to paddle each of these craft, there would have been
at least 600 of them, and the entire population would have exceeded 2,400. As a
final point, emphasis may be placed upon the opinion expressed by some secondary
historians (Ballard, 1866: p. 429; Hadley, 1903: p. 66) that the Pennacook had
previously been much more numerous than they were when found by the English.

We have the canoe figure of 2,400, Williamson's estimate of 3,000 souls, that of
Potter of 2,000, and the habitation site data, which suggests 3,200. The arithmetical
average is 2,650. It will be conservative, therefore, to accept 2,500 as the population
of the Merrimac River Pennacook at or shortly before A. D. 1600.

### THE WINNEPESAUKEE

The group is described by Hodge (1910: Part II, p. 962) as a Pennacook band
located on Lake Winnepesaukee. The relationship may have been close politically to
the Pennacook on the Merrimac, but geographically it was distinct. Our evidence

concerning occupation around the lake is derived principally from archaeological reconnaissance. On the basis of this evidence Day (1962: p. 29) has expressed the opinion that the Winnepesaukee region "may have been one of the most populous centers in New England."

Moorehead (1931) surveyed the water courses from Franklin to the lake and found nine village sites on the lake, of which seven were in the southwest corner. Since these were all late habitation sites, not temporary camp sites or burial grounds, it is reasonable to suppose that they were simultaneously occupied. Some may have been quite large, with perhaps 200-250 inhabitants. Others are sure to have been smaller, but few are likely to have held less than 15 wigwams, or 100 persons. If we use the smallest probable average, 125 persons, the total for the group is 1,125.

Moorehead's party also surveyed the lower reaches of the Pemigewasset River, a Merrimac tributary. He found four village sites. Since these may have been more remote than those previously discussed, and since their occupancy may have been intermittent, we may ascribe to them an average population of 100 inhabitants. The total number for these, then, is 400.

Some confirmation comes from Price (1967: pp. 3, 10). He mentions a village at Franklin, which may have been one of Moorehead's sites; one at "The Weirs" at the outlet of Lake Winnepesaukee; and one at Moultonborough Neck. In addition he mentions two at or near Alton Bay in the southeast corner of the lake. All of these may well be included among Moorehead's 13 sites, but it must be realized that Price was more interested in locating trails than in naming villages, and that those villages he does mention were well established in early colonial times. In connection with the villages at Alton Bay he comments that, judging by the number of artifacts found, the region was heavily occupied. Our estimate for the entire Pemigewasset-Winnepesaukee area is 1,525, or let us round it off to 1,500.

## THE COOSUC

The territory to the north and west of the Merrimac Basin and Lake Winnepesaukee was occupied by people whose political affinities lay with the Pennacook Confederacy. According to Hodge (1907: Part I, p. 342) this band was small, "probably Pennacook," and had its village at the junction of the Ammonoosuc River and the Connecticut. Their village may have been located at this point, but their activity extended through Coos and Grafton counties. They are mentioned by Barstow (1842: p. 22) as being in Grafton County and on the Connecticut River. Kidder (1859: p. 236) called them Cowasack, and placed them on the upper Connecticut. Price says (1967: p. 4) that the Indian village of "Cossuck" was at Newbury, on the Vermont side of the river; that there was a camping place at East Barnet, Vermont; and "probably" a village at Lyme, New Hampshire.

It is likely that the Coosuc, or at least the Indians who lived in New Hampshire north of the 44th parallel, possessed more than a single village. However, in this rough and wild country, they may well have maintained their permanent headquarters in only one central spot. If so, their focus was at the village near Newbury, and it must have been quite large. An estimate of 300 persons will not exaggerate the size of that band, which wandered over nearly 100 miles of the upper Connecticut.

## VERMONT AND WESTERN NEW HAMPSHIRE

This large expanse of territory contained relatively few inhabitants. Indeed, some historians have felt that there were almost none at all. Day (1962: p. 28) has expressed this point of view emphatically. He says in part: ". . . historians have generally treated Vermont as an uninhabited area. Ethnographically it has been a virtual *terra incognita.* There does not seem to be, either in print or in manuscript, a single account of any group settled within the entire area prior to King Philip's War."

Two factors probably conduce to this vacuum in our knowledge. The first is the nature of the land itself. Apart from the Connecticut River and Lake Champlain there was no open river valley which could furnish fish and provide level land for planting. The forested hills and mountains were valuable principally for game, the taking of which required roving, nomadic, hunting techniques, but which did not favor the presence of sedentary villages. The second factor is that the European settlement in its early days adhered to the coast and penetrated slowly up the major rivers. The entry into the rough interior came therefore so late that the natives already had died from disease and war, or had moved elsewhere. Ruttenber (1872: p. 80) pointed to the essential facts very clearly when he said: "Had the lands upon which they were located been sold in small tracts and opened to settlement at an early period, they would not have escaped observation and record; but the wilderness was a sealed book for many years, and there are those who still write that it was without Indian habitations."

Recent archaeologists and ethnographers have maintained that Vermont was the home of settled Indians in the past, but this controversy has concerned primarily the region of Lake Champalin (see Perkins, 1909: p. 607; Sherman, 1941; Huden, 1960, 1962; and Richie, 1961: p. 251), and is therefore not pertinent to a description of the Pennacook.

With respect to the Connecticut Valley the situation is somewhat different. The Squawkeag and Pocumtuc were located in the Connecticut and Deerfield valleys in the extreme southeastern corner of Vermont and the southwestern corner of New Hampshire. However, these tribes are better considered in association with the Massachusetts Indians below the state line (see pp. 56-58). Above the Squawkeag, Huden (1962) assigns the Connecticut Valley on both sides to the Pennacook as far north as the Coosuc and says: "Traces of these peaceful people indicate that they lived in considerable numbers in Windham and Windsor Counties, Vermont." Although "considerable numbers" may mean almost anything, we cannot envision many Indians who lived permanently on the river, and there is no record of any permanent villages above the Squawkeag at Hinsdale, New Hampshire. Hence we estimate a population of no more than 100 along the stretch of river between Hinsdale and the Coosuc territory.

The remainder of western New Hampshire was inhabited, but sparsely. The best local habitat was offered by Lake Sunapee, where a permanent village of some size appears to have existed (Price, 1967: p. 11). Many camp grounds have been found between the Merrimac and the Connecticut, a fact which implies a good deal of moving about through the region, even if there were but few established villages.

The settlement at Newbury (Lake Sunapee) may be allowed, plus two or three smaller villages elsewhere. The total might come to 300 inhabitants but is not likely to have been greater.

## THE OSSIPEE, PEQUAKET, AND NEWICHAWANOC

A region southeast of the White Mountains extends along the New Hampshire-Maine border from Conway to Berwick and embraces Ossipee Lake and River, the headwaters of the Saco River, the Salmon Falls River, and most of the middle Piscataqua. Prior to 1620 it was the home of at least three recognizable small tribes or bands, the Ossipee, the Pequaket, and the Newichawanoc. With regard to their ethnic affiliation as well as their specific habitat, there is some confusion among historians and ethnographers.

The Ossipee, according to Hodge (1910: Part II, p. 161) were a small tribe belonging to the Pennacook Confederacy, who lived on Lake Ossipee and in Oxford County, Maine. Morse (1822: p. 67) placed them on the Saco, but Barstow (1842: p. 22) said that they were on both Lakes Ossipee and Winnepesaukee. Sylvester (1910: Vol. 2, p. 42) said that the Ossipee inhabited the wilds about the lake, and Price (1967: p. 2) agrees with him. Swanton (1952: p. 14) lists them under the Abnaki and locates them on Lake Ossipee. It is probable that the tribe occupied all the territory to the northeast of Lake Winnepesaukee and maintained its center of gravity at and about Lake Ossipee. Whether or not it should be included under the Pennacook or the Abnaki is more or less irrelevant here because we are interested primarily in numbers, not tribal relationships.

The Pequaket, it is agreed by all authorities, lived on the upper Saco River and had their principal, if not their only, village at what is now Fryeburg, Maine. Their ethnic affiliation seems to have been definitely with the Abnaki.

Concerning the Newichawanoc there is more uncertainty. They lived on the Piscataqua River and extended downstream certainly as far as Berwick, Maine, but there is no indication that they reached the sea. Northward, according to Hodge (1910: Part II, p. 65), they reached the "upper" Piscataqua. Williamson (1839: Vol. 1, p. 458) mentions them as a tribe on the upper branches of that river. They seem to have belonged to the Pennacook Confederacy, and are listed as such by Swanton (1952: p. 18), who places them on the upper Piscataqua and the Salmon Falls Rivers. Thus they must have impinged upon the Ossipee at the southern limit of the latter.

With respect to population, the best-known statement is that by Morse (1822: p. 67), who says he derived his figures from Williamson, but the latter author does not cite the same figures in his principal work, *The History of the State of Maine,* edition of 1839. At any rate, for the year 1616, Morse gives 1,000 persons for the Newichawanoc on the Piscataqua together with the Ossipee tribes on the Saco. There were also a maximum of 400 Pequaket at Fryeburg. The total is 1,400 souls.

For the Pequaket there is a very good contemporary estimate, reported in Winthrop's *Journal,* (1630-49: Vol. 2, p. 62): Darby Field, on his trip in 1642 to climb Mt. Washington, passed through the Indian village at Fryeburg. He said there were 200 people there — considerably less than 400 — but the latter figure may have included the whole tribe. Further confirmation comes from a statement cited by Hodge (1910: Part II, p. 229) with reference to the battle of 1725 between these Indians and the English. There were 80 Indians, "the entire force of the tribe." Under such conditions the entire population may have amounted to about 300. If we allow for attrition between 1616 and 1725, we may be reasonably confident that at the former date the population reached 400. If this is true it is equally likely that Williamson's estimate (through Morse) of 1,000 for the combined Ossipee and Newichawanoc is valid.

Another avenue of approach is through the villages known or recorded for the area. That of the Pequaket at Fryeburg has already been discussed. The Pequaket, as far as is known, had no other village. The Newichawanoc are stated by Hodge (1910: Part II, p. 65) and others to have had their principal village at Berwick, Maine, but Price (1967: p. 3) an archaeologist who has examined exhaustively the historic Indian trails of New Hampshire, and who is thoroughly familiar with local detail, writes: "The 'Newij-wan-ok' . . . trail began at tidewater below 'Kwam-pi-gon' . . . and Newichwannok, both villages being located in what is now South Berwick, Maine." If there were two villages, both in the same modern township, they must be regarded as constituting a single aggregate of population, although probably an unusually large one. The principal village of the Ossipee was on the western shore of the lake and is described by Price (1967: p. 2) as "large."

These groups, then, had three villages, all well authenticated and all of sizable proportions. That of the Pequaket has been estimated as having had 400 inhabitants in 1616. The others can scarcely have been much smaller. If, however, we allow them 300 each, the total is 1,000.

In addition, other villages of a permanent nature probably existed in the same region. Price (1967: p. 1) has come on some of these which are worth consideration. He points out that "the locations of the many Indian villages played an important part in the routes chosen for the early Indian trails," and then goes on to mention several which flourished until the epidemic, or plague of 1616-1618, and which thereafter were abandoned. Among these were "Kchi-tegu," or Chataguay near Conway in Ossipee territory, the Suncook village near Gilmanton Iron Works, and "Pisgatock" near Somersworth, not far from Berwick, Maine. These may have been small places; we have no means for estimating their size. Consequently they may be considered to have had a population of 100 persons each. The total of six villages, therefore, reaches 1,300, a figure almost identical with that given by Williamson (1839: Vol. I, p. 465) and by Morse (1822: p. 67). Since all the prehistoric villages are not now known, either 1,300 or 1,400 seems a reasonable, if not conservative, estimate. Let us say 1,400.

## THE ACCOMINTA AND PISCATEQUA

The Accominta are described by Hodge (1907: Part I, p. 8) as a small tribe or band of the Pennacook Confederacy with a village at or near York, Maine. Williamson (1839: Vol. I, p. 457) said that they were the last group before one reached the Abnaki. The Piscatequa, according to Hodge (1910: Part II, p. 262) were like-wise a small tribe connected with the Pennacook. Their home was near Dover, New Hampshire. They were mentioned by Hubbard (1680: pp. 31-34) as a "society" existing between the Saco and the Merrimac, and by Swanton (1952: p. 18) as a village of the Pennacook.

Both tribes were in the list of "countries" compiled by Captain John Smith (1616: p. 5). In the *Description of New England* he mentions five of these entities which lie between the Abnaki and the Massachusetts. The second and third, respectively, are Accominticus (Accominta) at York, Maine, and Passataquack (Piscatequa) at Dover, New Hampshire. Their existence seems, therefore, to be firmly established.

With regard to their population, these tribes have been referred to as small, and I can find no evidence of more than a single village pertaining to each. John Smith's account is of little help for he merely includes the Accominta and the Piscatequa in a list. On the other hand, the fact that he designated them "countries" is an indication that they were of some importance. Located in the favorable coastal habitat, they may have reached 250 persons each. Five hundred for the two tribes does not seem excessive.

### THE NASHUA, SOUHEGAN, AND WACHUSETT

After having made a wide detour to the east, we return to the Merrimac River tribes, beginning with those who adjoined the Pennacook proper to the south. The principal one of these was the Nashua, but two other bands require comment: the Souhegan and the Wachusett. The Souhegan were undoubtedly a branch of the Pennacook. According to Hodge (1910: Part II, p. 617) they lived on the Souhegan River, Hillsborough County, New Hampshire, probably at Amherst, a place originally called Souhegan. Hodge elsewhere (1910: Part II, p. 225) lists the Souhegan as one of the tribes directly composing the Pennacook Confederacy. Their connection with the Nashua was close. Price (1967: p. 7) says that the latter tribe had cornfields in the Souhegan Valley. The size of their village is not stated to have been large, but it seems to have possessed some importance. Its population may be estimated as 200 persons.

As we descend the Merrimac Valley we next encounter the Nashua River, which flows in from the south. Its banks were inhabited by the Nashua, and, to the north-west, the Wachusett. The latter tribe possessed a village near Mt. Wachusett at Princeton, Massachusetts. The location, ethnic affiliation, and villages of both tribes have been the cause of much disagreement. Both have been assigned to the Pennacook (Hodge, 1910: Part II, p. 33; Swanton, 1952: p. 35), the Nipmuck (Ellis and Morris, 1906: p. 18; Gahan, 1941), and the Massachusetts (Sylvester, 1910: Vol. 1, p. 51). The principal village of the Nashua has been variously placed at Leominster (Hodge, 1910: Part II, p. 33), at Lancaster (Gookin, 1674: p. 193; Price, 1967: p. 7), and at Sterling, Massachusetts (Willard, 1826: p. 290). According to Price (1967: p. 7), they also had a small village at Nashua, New Hampshire. There has been confusion among writers between Nashua, New Hampshire, and Nashoba,

Massachusetts. The details of the controversy cannot occupy us here to the exclusion of demographic data.

With regard to population several points emerge from the contradictory statements which have come down to us. First, the Nashua, and with them the Wachusett, appear once to have been numerous. Gookin (1674: p. 193) refers to them as a "people" living at Weshakin and says they "have been a great people in former times." Second, prior to King Philip's War, they had been badly mauled by the Mohawk, to whose attacks they were exposed for years. Gahan (1941) says that "the Nashuas were reduced in a generation from a relatively powerful band to a remnant, but eighteen families being left at their principal village, Washacum, at Sterling. The Mohawks destroyed Wachusett at Princeton, compelled the abandonment of Nashoba, and continually raided and killed."

The reference to Washacum is probably derived from Gookin (1674: p. 193), who said that there were not above fifteen or sixteen surviving families. Willard (1826: p. 290), in quoting Gookin, says that this author probably referred to the settlement at Washacum alone, an opinion with which Gahan concurs. Willard also quotes Gookin as saying that "this miserable remnant" was wasting away when he saw them.

Hodge (1910: Part II, p. 33) says that after King Philip's War (1675-1676) the Nashua "numbering several hundred" attempted to escape in two parties, of which "a large number" were killed or captured. Afterward 200 crossed the Hudson River, while "a few" joined the Pennacook, and "a few" returned to their old home. The interpretation of these statements by the writer in the *Handbook* that the Nashua after King Philip's War consisted of several hundred persons is undoubtedly erroneous, for most of the Indians who were seeking to escape were Nipmuck, not Nashua. Nevertheless, these claims, together with the undeniable participation of the Nashua as strong allies of Philip, and the relatively high position held by their chief sagamore Sam, are not in accord with the earlier debilitation ascribed to the tribe by Gookin and others. It is probable that the accounts of these writers reflect the condition of the tribe after Philip's War, rather than before. At the same time there is little doubt that the Mohawk raids occurred and that the Nashua, with the Wachusett, had suffered severe losses in the years between 1630 and 1675. The evidence as a whole supports Gookin's assertion that the tribe toward the end of the seventeenth century was almost wasted away, but had once been of considerable size.

The known villages of the Nashua and the Wachusett included the main settlement at Washacum; a smaller village at Nashua, New Hampshire, or at Nashoba, Massachusetts; and a village at Wachusett. The latter may be considered to have held 200 people. The settlement at Washacum was clearly large, and may be estimated at 300 persons. The third village may be put at 200. The total population would then have reached 700, without allowance for smaller, unrecorded settlements. An attrition of 200 referable to Mohawk raids and disease would have brought the number to 500 in 1675. The calamity of King Philip's War could have destroyed or dispersed 400, leaving about 100 survivors. The assumed precontact population is not inconsistent with the numbers of participants, casualties, fugitives, and survivors recorded for the period 1675-1676.

## THE LOWER MERIMMAC RIVER

Along the Merrimac below the entrace of the Nashua River lived a number of Pennacook subtribes, or bands, which have been noted by both Hodge (1910: Part II, p. 225) and Swanton (1952: p. 18), as well as by older writers. Of these the largest was probably the Wamesit. They are described by Hodge as being a tribe and village of the Pennacook Confederacy located on the south bank of the Merrimac below the entrance of the Concord River. The village was near Lowell. Swanton (1952: p. 18) gives the same information but calls the Wamesit a division of the Pennacook. The second tribe was the Pentucket, which, according to Hodge (1910: Part II, p. 227) and to Williamson (1839: Vol. 1, p. 458) originally had their village at Haverhill, Massachusetts. Williamson places them on the Merrimac at Dracut, Massachusetts. The third band was the Squamscot, who apparently lived on the Exeter River, near Exeter, New Hampshire. The fourth was the Winnecowet, a small tribe who lived somewhere in Rockingham County, New Hampshire.

The Wamesit were described by Gookin (1674: pp. 148-149) under the name of Pawtucket. They were, he says, over the Pennacook and several other groups. He ascribes, apparently to all of these bands, a total of 3,000 men, a number which would mean a population of 12,000. However, he adds: "But these were almost totally destroyed by the great sickness." He also states that in 1674 there were not above 250 men, besides women and children, an aggregate of possibly 800-1,000 souls. Here he may have been referring to all the tribes along the Merrimac. Nevertheless this was in 1674, and the Wamesit made a substantial contribution to King Philip's forces during the war of the next two years. After the war, although they had suffered severely, there were enough left to sell their land in 1686 and move to St. Francis. At least a few hundred must have been alive before the war, and although Gookin's 250 men for the Wamesit may have been an overestimate, it may also indicate the correct order of magnitude. If we allow 200 men and 750 souls in 1674, the aboriginal population must have been much greater. Tentatively we may say that the attrition due to plague and other causes amounted to 50 percent of the precolonial number. Then the original population may have reached 1,500.

The Pentucket village at Haverhill, according to Hodge (1910: Part II, p. 227), was sold to the whites in 1642. If this sale occurred only 12 years after the first Massachusetts Bay towns were founded, it argues an early and complete disintegration of the band, one which would most likely have been caused by epidemic. The Pentucket are mentioned by Hubbard (1680: pp. 31-34) as a group within the Merrimac "society." Later Williamson (1839: p. 458) says that the Pentucket were on the Merrimac with their principal village at the falls at Dracut, which "it is said once had 3,000 souls." These statements are difficult to reconcile unless we allow the existence of two villages, one at Haverhill, the other at Dracut. Both

disappeared very early in the colonial period. In view of their rapid disintegration
the population of each may be put at 200, a total of 400 for the tribe.

Regarding Squamscot the only information which has come to my attention
is a statement by Hodge (1910: Part II, p. 629) that this was "a part of the Pennacook Confederacy, called a tribe, which formerly lived on Exeter River, probably
about the present site of Exeter." Swanton (1952: p. 18) lists the band under the
Pennacook, and Price (1967: p. 8) merely refers to a place on the southern Pentucket Trail "called Squamscott by the colonists, and now Exeter." It was a place
for salmon fishing and may have been no more than a camp ground. However, in
view of its persistence as the name of a tribe, or band, it is legitimate to assume
that there was a settlement of some kind at Squamscot, and that it probably took
the form of a permanent village. The population may have been moderate, not
exceeding 150 souls.

Winnecowet was another group noted by Hodge (1910: Part II, p. 962). His
only authority for its inclusion is a reference to Potter in Schoolcraft's *Archives
of Aboriginal Knowledge.* This lack of contemporary sources is also true of Squamscot. Winnecowet is said to have been located in Rockingham County, New
Hampshire, but where within the county is unknown. Its existence is dubious;
nevertheless, the tradition of the name and its persistence at least to the mid-
nineteenth century argues for some sort of settlement. Largely as speculation we
may assign an aboriginal population of 100 souls to the tribe.

In summary, for the lower Merrimac area we have the Wamesit, with 1,500
estimated population, Pentucket with 400, Squamscot with 150, and Winnecowet
with 100. The total is 2,150 souls.

The region occupied by these four small bands embraces the drainage of the
Merrimac River from just above Lowell to a point between Amesbury and Newburyport, Massachusetts; the drainages of the Concord River below North Sudbury,
Massachusetts; of the Shawsheen River complete; of the upper half of the Ipswich
River; and of the upper two-thirds of the Exeter River in New Hampshire. This
region has been subjected to exhaustive investigation by local archaeologists, notably
Moorehead (1931) and Bullen (1941, 1949), who have located and plotted on
maps most of the prehistoric Indian sites. It is both interesting and significant to
examine their data with the purpose of comparing population estimated according
to settlement density with that derived from recorded history.

From the map of Bullen (1941) it is clear that, apart from the coast, Indian
habitation throughout Massachusetts, and no doubt in New Hampshire also, was
concentrated along the main streams or was relatively close to them. Therefore the
river surveys would find most of the permanent settlements, although some would
be located on nearby lakes. Let us look at some of the surveys of the lower Merrimac tributaries.

Moorehead published his site maps in the paper entitled *The Merrimack
Archaeological Survey* (1931). In figures 16 and 17 he shows 14 village sites,
as opposed to shell heaps and camp grounds, on the Concord River from two miles
above the junction of the Concord with the Merrimac down to North Sudbury, a

distance of about 20 miles as the stream flows. The average is one site every 1.4 river miles. Over this same stretch Bullen (1941, map) shows a concentration of dots along the river and up to four miles laterally, where each dot represents a site of some kind, not differentiated according to type. However, even if the majority depict some quite temporary activity such as fishing, the density of residues along the stream indicate a relatively heavy occupation of the area, one which continued until contact times.

On the Shawsheen River, which runs into the Merrimac near Lawrence, Bullen (1941) on his generalized map of Massachusetts, shows numerous sites. On the upper half of the Ipswich he shows the sites equally thick. Approximately 30 miles of river are included on his map. In a later paper (1949: p. 4) Bullen gives another map, this one of only the Shawsheen and the upper seven miles of the Ipswich. Here the dots that represent sites are clearly graded according to size. There are close to 65 in all, of which seven are of the largest category and may be assumed to stand for permanent village sites. If the stream distances are taken as 22 miles, the average is nearly one permanent site for every three miles of river.

Along the Merrimac itself Moorehead surveyed from central New Hampshire to the sea. According to his maps, from Tyngsborough to Newburyport, a distance of 40 miles, there are 26 major village sites, including one in the township of Salem, New Hampshire. The average is one village per 1.5 river miles. On Bullen's map of Massachusetts (1941) the number of dots denoting sites reaches a density along the Merrimac comparable with that found along the Concord.

For the Exeter River no data are given by either Bullen or Moorehead, but if we consider the length of the stream as 15 miles, and use the findings for the other rivers, we may estimate that Moorehead would have found ten village sites (at 1.5 miles per site). The totals for all the streams investigated, plus the Exeter River, are 97 miles and 57 sites.

These values may be recomputed for area. The streams are relatively small and rather evenly spaced through the territory. Although habitation was confined quite strictly to the stream banks, the land of the entire watersheds was utilized. The region drained, with all tributaries, by the lower Merrimac, the lower half of the Concord, the upper half of the Ipswich, the Shawsheen, and the upper two-thirds of the Exeter, amounts to somewhere near 850 square miles, as determined from a standard map with a polar planimeter. Since the boundaries of the watersheds are necessarily more or less vague, we may say that the area falls within the range of 800 to 900 square miles. If there were 57 village sites the density would be almost 15 square miles per site.

For demographic purposes it is not enough to know the number and distribution of sites discovered by modern archaeologists. One must also have a fair idea of, first, the average size, or population, and, second, the proportion of settlement areas which were simultaneously inhabited. With regard to the latter factor, as pointed out previously, archaeologists and prehistorians vary in their estimates but agree that within hunter-gatherer cultures, even those of a semiagricultural nature, only a portion of the later identified sites were occupied at the same time.

In the discussion of the Pennacook proper, embracing the middle and upper Merrimac, we considered that the principal sites found by archaeologists such as Moorehead and Marshall represented permanent subdivisions of the Pennacook. This conclusion was reached because there was reasonable correspondence between documentary and archaeological data for the region north of Manchester. It is probably not wise to extend this principle to the lower Merrimac system. Nevertheless, it will be justifiable to regard at least one-third of Moorehead's village sites on the lower Merrimac and Concord rivers as the homes of substantial bodies of Indians at the beginning of the seventeenth century. To these may be added an equivalent number calculated by river-mile from the Shawsheen, the Ipswich, and the Exeter rivers. The total is 57, of which one-third would be 19.

With regard to size, we have considered that the principal village of a tribe or band held 250 or even 300 persons, and that well-populated centers such as that of the Pennacook on the Merrimac contained 200 souls. Smaller, ordinary villages would have had 100 each. The area under consideration once was occupied by four tribal groups. Each might have had one village of 250 persons. Of the other 15, five might have had 200, the rest 100. This estimate would yield a total of 3,000 souls — much higher than that based upon documentary evidence, which reached only 2,150.

Obviously there is considerable discrepancy between the two methods. I incline to give greater credence to the archaeological data, and this for two reasons. In the first place, there is an almost complete lack of solid historical evidence concerning this region in the early seventeenth century. In the second place, it is known that some of the tribes disintegrated, sold their lands, and disappeared only a few years after the settlement of Massachusetts Bay. This demoralization would have been possible only as the result of severe epidemics. We may therefore assess the population of the four tribes and of the territory they occupied at 3,000 persons.

## THE AGAWAM AND NAUMKEAG

These two bands were the only divisions of the Pennacook who were settled on the coast rather than upon inland streams. The Agawam were located at or near Ipswich, the Naumkeag at Salem. Both were known to and mentioned by Captain John Smith (1616: p. 5) and by Hubbard (1680: pp. 31-34). The former writer called them "countries," the latter "societies." They were also mentioned, although not by name, by earlier explorers who ran along the Massachusetts coast, and who universally described them at that time as very numerous. However, they had almost disappeared by the 1630's, when only a few score seem to have survived. The cause of their collapse may in part have been due to incursions by the Tarratines (Abnaki) of Maine, for reports of intertribal warfare are very numerous, but seem mostly to have been referable to the plague of 1616-1618. This epidemic, which certainly almost wiped out the neighboring Massachusetts, and which devasted far up the Merrimac, probably nearly destroyed the Agawam and the Naumkeag. In any event, their former size can only be inferred from the prominence accorded them by Smith and others. If each band possessed only one village it must have been quite large. More likely there were at least two villages and perhaps more at both Ipswich and Salem. If so, we may estimate the tribal population to have been 500 each, or 1,000 jointly.

The archaeological data are rather unsatisfactory. Bullen (1941), on his distribution map of sites in Massachusetts, shows a heavy concentration from the mouth of the Merrimac southward to the base of Cape Ann. The sites reached a high density on Plum Island, probably referable to extensive shell middens. There are seven sites shown near Annisquam, and five at Salem. Otherwise there is a total blank from the mouth of the Ipswich River to that of the Charles. This apparent gap cannot be taken as a real phenomenon. It is probably due simply to a lack of surveys along this stretch of coast. However, regardless of the reason, Bullen's map is rendered useless as a guide to Indian settlement.

Moorehead (1931: fig. 5) shows clearly 16 village sites between the mouth of the Merrimac and that of the Ipswich. Three are close to the coast at Newburyport, three are on Plum Island, and the rest are scattered to the interior. They all lie in the territory of the Agawam. If we follow the previous example and count one-third of the sites as simultaneously occupied, say six, with an average population of 150 persons, we get a total of 900 for the Agawam. The Naumkeag would have been as numerous, and the aggregate for the two tribes would be 1,800. This figure far exceeds the conjecture based upon documentary sources. In this case we may seek a compromise and take the approximate average, 1,500 souls.

## DISCUSSION AND CONCLUSIONS

The survey of the Pennacook Confederacy and its allies has now been completed. Included is the entire population of New Hampshire, together with most of Essex County, Massachusetts, and a little of Maine. The findings, according to tribal name may be summarized as follows.

| | | | |
|---|---|---|---|
| Pennacook proper | 2,500 | Accominta, Piscatequa | 500 |
| Winnepesaukee | 1,500 | Nashua, Souhegan, Wachusett | 700 |
| Coosuc | 300 | The lower Merrimac | 3,000 |
| Vermont & western | | Agawam, Naumkeag | 1,500 |
| New Hampshire | 300 | | |
| Ossipee, Pequaket, Newichawanoc | 1,400 | Total | 11,700 |

Let us round it off to 12,000 souls.

This figure is far beyond the limits ordinarily allotted to the Pennacook and other tribes in the area, and yet it is very difficult to see how it can be much reduced. The following points should be considered.

1. The total is of the same order of magnitude as that claimed by Gookin (1674: pp. 148-149): 3,000 men, or 12,000 souls. Krzywicki (1934: p. 518) says that probably Gookin meant 3,000 persons, not "men," but Gookin is absolutely explicit, and he was more familiar than most of his contemporaries with Indian population.

2. Mooney and Thomas (Hodge, *Handbook,* 1910: Part II, p. 226) list 17 villages and bands as comprising the Pennacook Confederacy. To these must be

added the inhabitants of the Connecticut Valley above the Massachusetts line, and those in southwestern New Hampshire, making in effect 18 groups. If each of these contained 300 persons, and no tribe or band or other named body could maintain continuous, independent, organized existence with fewer members, the aggregate is 5,400. Some of the 18 groups must have contained much more than 300 persons, yet Mooney (1928: p. 4) allows only 2,000 for all these entities, which he lists under the name Pennacook.

3. As noted at the outset of this discussion of the Pennacook, Mooney and Thomas (Hodge, 1910: Part II, p. 225) concede that the Confederacy had been reduced to 2,500 in 1630 and to 1,250 in 1674. They consider smallpox responsible, but it is more likely that the initial lethal agent was the plague of 1616-1618. In other areas the plague destroyed better than 90 percent of the population. Here it may not have been so severe, yet if we add also the casualties attending other epidemics and newly introduced diseases, it becomes possible to estimate the loss as reaching 75 percent of the original number. Then, if 2,500 were left in 1630, there would once have been 10,000. In particular the coastal tribes, the Agawam and the Naumkeag, were almost extirpated and those of the lower and middle Merrimac suffered heavily.

4. The archaeological pattern, as demonstrated by Marshall, Moorehead, and Bullen, for the heart of the Pennacook territory, displays an intensive occupation by native communities. The water courses, the coasts, the accessible lands of the interior, were all fully developed up to the carrying capacity of the area for the type of culture and technology of the inhabitants. The estimates here offered for the size and distribution of simultaneously occupied villages may depart from the actuality to a considerable degree in detail, but the broad picture must be one of an active, viable economy, which could support a population much larger than was seen by the Puritans in the middle of the seventeenth century.

5. It has been noted previously that the province of the lower Merrimac River and its feeder streams encompassed an area of roughly 850 square miles. In this region we estimate that there lived 3,000 persons. The density therefore, is about 3.5 persons per square mile. The entire Pennacook Confederacy embraced a much larger territory. It included, as envisaged here, all of New Hampshire south of Coos County; the Saco Valley in Maine; and Essex County plus part of Middlesex in Massachusetts. These limits contained much marginal land and great tracts of wilderness. Hence the density of habitation would be relatively low. The area considered extended approximately 9,600 square miles and if our figures are correct supported close to 12,000 people. The density would then be approximately 1.25 persons per square mile. Both the restricted and the extended densities are entirely reasonable under the circumstances.

All these factors conduce to the conclusion that the population of the Pennacook and their allies reached the bracket of 10,000 to 15,000 in the year 1600, with a likely middle value of 12,000.

# Chapter 3

# SOUTHEASTERN MASSACHUSETTS AND THE ISLANDS

## THE MASSACHUSETTS

Unlike the Pennacook, the Massachusetts constituted a homogeneous tribe, with several subordinate chieftaincies but no ethnically recognized subdivisions. They occupied the land and possessed numerous villages along the coast from just below the Naumkeag at Salem to the point of contact with the Wampanoag somewhere north of Plymouth. In addition they held the hinterland with villages in the watershed of the Charles and Neponset rivers. Their territory was not large, but they appear once to have been a strong, compact people.

Their aboriginal population must have been considerable if the testimony of those who encountered them has value as evidence. Although the Massachusetts were seen by and were known to many explorers during the sixteenth and early seventeenth centuries, only two of these have left detailed descriptions, Samuel Champlain and Captain John Smith, both men of keen observation and outstanding reliability.

Champlain passed along the coast in 1605 (see his *Voyages* in the 1907 edition, p. 67). He found Boston Harbor to be in an area which was heavily cultivated and well populated. He says that while he was there 15 or 16 canoes came out to his ship, some with as many as 15 or 16 persons aboard. If other canoes held fewer, the average complement must have been at least 10, and the total, 150 persons, undoubtedly all men. Such a showing immediately implies a population of fully 600 souls. It is to be assumed that these Indians came from miles around, but on the other hand not all the men would have been aboard the canoes. If as many stayed ashore as embarked in the canoes, an aggregate of well over 1,000 souls would have been represented. An additional note was contributed by Lescarbot (1612: Vol. 3, p. 95), who was with Champlain on his expedition. He refers in general terms to the Indians of the Massachusetts coast: "The Armouchiquois are a great people . . . this insolency proceeds from the strength given them by their numbers."

Captain John Smith was in Massachusetts Bay in 1616. His famous description is worth quoting in full (1616; in Force's *Tracts,* 1838, Vol. 2, p. 15):

> *The Isles of Mattahunts* are on the West side of this Bay, where are many Isles. . . . and then the Countrie of the Massachusetts, which is the Paradise of all these parts: for heere are many Isles all planted with corne: . . . The Sea Coast as you passe, shews you all along large corne fields, and great troupes of well proportioned people: but the French having remained heere neere sixe weekes, left nothing for us to take occasion to examine the inhabitants relations, viz. if there be neere three thousand people upon these Iles. . . .

Several writers who lived after 1620, and who learned about the Massachusetts from Indians and from other white men, emphasized the large Indian population

of the Boston Bay region. Of these the best known is Daniel Gookin, whose principal work, written in 1674 just before King Philip's War was published by the
Massachusetts Historical Society in 1792. According to him (pp. 148-149) the
Massachusetts could "in former time, arm for war, about three thousand men, as
the old Indians declare."

This figure, 3,000 men, has caused endless discussion. Taken at its face value,
it means a population of nearly 12,000 souls, in this instance an apparent absurdity.
Some students, e.g., Krzywicki (1934: p. 518) and Hodge (1907: Part I, p. 816),
have suggested that Gookin really meant 3,000 persons rather than warriors.
Others, such as Drake (1851: p. 106), merely quote Gookin without criticism. As
Gookin states, he accepted the word of Indians who had survived from ca. 1615
to ca. 1670. Their memory and their accuracy undoubtedly left much to be desired.
It is also of interest to note how the value 3,000 men crops up repeatedly with
reference to several New England tribal groups. In addition to the Massachusetts
we find it given for the Pennacook and the Wampanoag. Sometimes the figure becomes 4,000, as for the Pequot and the Narragansett. It seems almost as if the
Indians had developed a formula for conveying the idea of a great many people,
and used it when questioned by white men concerning former populations. Whether
this speculation has or has not merit, it is clear that although Gookin may have
transmitted the estimate in good faith, its source is suspect and we had best accept
it only with serious reservation.

Krzywicki (1934: p. 458) says that the Massachusetts consisted politically of
three sagamoreships and seven petty sagamoreships, but he cites no reference for
the statement. It may have come from Edward Johnson (1654: p. 66), who, in describing the effect of the plague, referred to the tribe "who were before this mortality most populous, having under them seven Dukedomes or petty Sagamores."
Some idea of the numbers controlled by a sagamore may be obtained from Higgeson
(1629: p. 50), who wrote: "The greatest Sagamores about us [near Plymouth] can
not make above three hundred men, but other lesse Saggamores have not above
fifteen subjects and others neere about us but two." If the "greatest" sagamores in
1629 headed 300 warriors, then at least the same number must be ascribed to the
seven who Johnson said had previously reigned over the Massachusetts. This calculation would give a total of 2,100 warriors, or approximately 8,000 persons. Krzywicki's statement would imply an even greater number, for the inference from Higgeson is that a "great" sagamore would once have commanded more than 300 men.

The fatal demographic blow to the Massachusetts was struck by the plague of
1617-1619, or, as it is sometimes given, 1616-1618. The nature of the malady need
not be discussed here, nor its effects throughout New England at large. Its relevance
depends upon the fact that it seems to have been particularly lethal to the Massachusetts and to the Wampanoag in the vicinity of Plymouth. At the risk of repeating
statements which have been quoted many times, we may review the testimony concerning the destruction of the Massachusetts.

The Englishman who was in the best position to evaluate the effect of the plague
was Captain John Smith, because he actually saw the tribe before the event. In 1622

(*New England's Trials* . . .: p. 12) he wrote: ". . . and this for advantage as they writ unto me, that God had laid this country open for us, and slaine the most part of the inhabitants by cruell warres and a mortall disease; for where I had seene 100 or 200 people, there is scarce ten to be found." Then he wrote that from Pembrocks Bay to Harrintons Bay there were not 20; from there to Cape Ann, some 30; from Taulbuts Bay to the River Charles, about 40. In other words, there were only about 90 Indians left along the entire Massachusetts coast north of Boston.

In 1631 (*Advertisements for the Inexperienced Planters* . . ., p. 16), Smith repeated essentially the same facts: "Not long after such a sicknesse came, that of five or six hundred about the Massachusetts there remained but thirty, on whom their neighbors fell and slew twenty eight." Again, he says: "But it is most certaine there was an exceeding great plague amonst them; for where I had seene two or three hundred, within three years after remained scarce thirty."

Others said much the same thing. John White (1630: p. 14) explained why the land was vacant: ". . . which comes to passe by the desolation hapning through a three yeares plague . . . which swept away most of the inhabitants all along the Sea coast, and in some places utterly consumed man, woman and childe, so that there is no person left to lay claime to the soyle which they possessed; In most of the rest, the Contagion hath scarce left alive one person of an hundred." Thomas Morton (1632: pp. 18-19) wrote a lurid account of the plague, in which he said that "in a place where many inhabited there hath been but one left alive," and in which he described "that Forrest, nere the Massachusetts" as a "new found Golgotha." Hubbard (1680: pp. 194-195) said that "the country of the Massachusetts, that was of all the Indians thereabouts the most populous, was in a manner upeopled by this disease." John Josselyn (1673: p. 294), referring to southeastern New England as a whole, wrote that the population was reduced from 30,000 to 3,000. His figures may be exaggerated, but the proportion of one survivor out of ten persons in the badly affected regions may be given credence.

Opinion is unanimous on the part of those present at or close to the visitation of the plague that, among the Massachusetts at least, the mortality was extraordinarily high. Estimates range from roughly 75 percent upward, with several flat assertions that in certain places all the inhabitants died. Such agreement in principle, even allowing for considerable latitude in detail, is rare. It must represent the essential fact that the overwhelming majority of the Massachusetts perished. If we wish to express the loss in numerical terms, we can discount total obliteration save for isolated spots, allow for pockets of survival, concede some exaggeration by the English writers, and conclude that a minimum of 75 percent of the tribe died between 1615 and 1620. The maximum value may well have been nearer 90 percent.

We must next consider the condition of the population which still remained during the decade 1620-1630. A great deal of illness persisted. As early as 1622 Winslow (1625: p. 250) visited the Massachusetts and found them suffering from disease. "When they came thither they found a great sickness to be amongst the Indians, not unlike the plague, if not the same." There are other accounts which mention the mortality suffered from chronic or acute respiratory diseases such as pneumonia and tuberculosis. It is very clear that the health of the native groups around Boston was rapidly deteriorating in this period.

As to population, Krzywicki (1934: p. 458) quotes Mooney and Thomas (in Hodge, 1907: Part I, p. 816), who, without citing their source, say that the Massachusetts numbered 500 in 1631. It is known, however, that in 1631 (Dudley, 1631: p. 6) the sachem Chickataubut on the Neponset River had 50-60 "subjects," and that John on the Mystic and John on the Saugus had 30-40 "men" each. These may be taken as 55, 35, and 35 respectively, or a total of 125 warriors. If we use a factor of four we get a population of 500, but this figure does not include substantial remnants on the Charles River. These would bring the aggregate well above the 500 mentioned by Hodge — let us say, to 750.

In 1633 a new disease, smallpox, almost annihilated the remainder of the Massachusetts around Boston Bay, although many in the interior survived to help form the villages of praying Indians which existed for many years at Natick, Nonantum, and Punkapog. Their number was suggested by Gookin (1674: p. 148), who said that "there are not of this people left at this day above three hundred men, besides women and children." This is an amazingly heavy population, and may well include members of other tribes who had gravitated to the missionary settlements. Regardless of the later condition of the Massachusetts, however, their strength in 1631 may be conservatively put at close to 750 souls.

It follows that if there were at least 750 alive in 1631, if these were the residue of a people, 75 to 90 percent of whom had died in the plague of 1617-1619, and if, during the preceding decade they had suffered further serious depletion due to disease, the original number must have reached a level far higher than that seen in 1631. The exact factor of decline is unknown, but it must have lain within the range of four to tenfold. The population in 1615 must therefore have attained a value of 3,000 to 7,500.

A somewhat different method of estimate is based upon the subtribal divisions and upon the villages known to have belonged to the Massachusetts. The former category has been discussed at length by Speck (1928b: pp. 94-105).

Speck equates control of territory, and hence population, with the names of several sachems or chieftains. The first and most important of these was Chickataubut, who held the lower Neponset and the entire district south of Boston. His son and grandson, both named Wampatuck, sold land at Quincy, Boston, and the North River, above Plymouth. The second chief was Nanepashanet, who controlled the land north of the Charles River, including Boston Harbor, Chelsea, Saugus, Lynn, and Marblehead. The third was a sachem named Manatahqua, who owned Nahant and Swampscott. The region east of the Concord River was controlled by a brother of Chickataubut. The fifth region was around Natick, where, prior to 1648, a sachem named Nahanton ruled. The sixth was the domain of Cutshamakin, another brother of Chickataubut, and included Dorchester, Sudbury, and Milton. To these Speck adds the names of two chiefs, Wittuwamet and Peksuot, the nature of whose holdings are unknown.

The size of these eight chiefdoms is not stated by Speck, although he imtimates that No. 1 was the largest, followed by No. 2. The seventh and eighth must have been very small, with the others intermediate in extent. It has been mentioned that in 1631 Chickataubut could still raise 50-60 men. Before the plague of 1617 the number must have been much greater. If the factor of reduction was only five, an original 1,000 people must have lived in the area. The second subtribe might have held 750; it was no doubt somewhat smaller than the domain of Chickataubut. The third, fourth, fifth, and sixth may be considered to have held 500 each, and the seventh and eighth 100 each. The total would have been close to 4,000.

With respect to villages, as opposed to subtribes or sagamoreships, Captain John Smith mentioned at least ten by name in his *Description of New England* (1616: p. 5), but the best summary is that in Hodge's *Handbook* (1907: Part I, p. 816) at the end of the article by Mooney and Thomas. Swanton (1952: pp. 19-20) lists 23 villages but adds nothing beyond what is said in the *Handbook* concerning individual places.

The list in the *Handbook* includes Naumkeag, which we have already considered as affiliated with the Pennacook, but it does not include Nahant, which certainly belonged to the Massachusetts. Of the remainder, Wonasquam was located at and may be synonymous with Annisquam. If so, it should be included with the coastal bands of the Pennacook. Six villages are recorded as inhabited by praying Indians. Whether they were aboriginally native habitations or, like Natick, were founded by John Eliot, Daniel Gookin, and their fellow missionaries, is not clear. If we delete them we have a residue of nineteen authentic villages, which are listed as follows.

*Conohasset.* Near Cohasset, sold in 1635. Mentioned by Smith (1616: p. 5).

*Massachusett.* Mentioned by Smith as the chief village. The location is uncertain. Hubbard (1680: pp. 194-195) says it was at or near the mouth of the Charles River.

*Mishawam.* At Charlestown. It was the home of a sagamore John in the early 1630's.

*Mystick.* At Medford. Winthrop (1630-49: Vol. 1, p. 114) says 30 persons died there of smallpox, but it was occupied in 1649.

*Nahant.* Mentioned by Drake (1867: p. 27). Speck (1928b: p. 102) says it belonged to chief Manatahqua.

*Nahapassumkeck.* In northern Plymouth County, on the coast. Mentioned by Smith (1616: p. 5).

*Nasnocomacack.* In northern Plymouth County, on the coast. Mentioned by Smith (1616: p. 5).

*Neponset.* An important village at Stoughton, Norfolk County. The home of Chickataubut.

*Nonantum.* At West Newton on the Charles River. The people later moved to Natick.

*Patuxet.* Near and north of Plymouth. This village was depopulated in 1617.

*Pocapawmet.* On the south shore of Massachusetts Bay. Seen by Smith in 1614.

*Sagoquas.* South of Cohasset. Mentioned by Smith (1616: p. 5).

*Saugus.* Near Lynn. The sagamore, John, died of smallpox in 1633.

*Seccasaw.* North shore of Plymouth County.

*Topeent.* North shore of Plymouth County. Mentioned by Smith (1616: p. 5).

*Totant.* Near Boston. Mentioned by Smith (1616: p. 5).

*Totheat.* North shore of Plymouth County. Mentioned by Smith (1616: p. 5).

*Wessagusset.* Near Weymouth.

*Winnesimmet.* At Chelsea. Drake (1867: p. 26) says it could raise 60 men. Suffered heavily from smallpox in 1633.

It will be noted that most of these villages are coastal. The exceptions are important centers on the Charles and Neponset rivers. If the Massachusetts built villages in the interior, their names and locations have been lost. In his discussion of tribal boundaries Speck (1928b: pp. 94ff.) carries the Massachusetts nearly to Concord and well beyond Framingham in the west. They met the Wampanoag somewhere at or beyond the headwaters of the Charles and Neponset rivers, roughly along the 42nd parallel. It is strange that this rather large area should have been devoid of permanent settlements, and yet there is no evidence of any villages in the contemporary literature. We are forced to assume that this region was used primarily for hunting and perhaps agriculture by the inhabitants of the coastal and riparian centers.

The size of the villages which survived in 1631 has already been indicated. From Governor Dudley's figures (1631: p. 6) for three of them, we have 55, 35, and 35 "men." The largest figure is supported by Drake (1867: p. 26), who says that the sachem of Neponset raised 60 warriors for an expedition, as did the sachem of Winnesimmet. If we reduce this number to 55 we get four villages with 55, 55, 35, and 35 warriors. The total is 180 men, or 720 souls, an average of 180 people per village. These may be taken as representing the largest villages, with the highest survival rate among the Massachusetts.

If four villages had an average of 180 persons in 1631, and the attrition due to warfare and the plague is assumed to have been only one-half, the number of inhabitants per village in 1615 must have reached 360, and may have been greater. If all the other towns were smaller — and we do not know that this was true — the overall average might have reached 200, and very likely 250. Then, with nineteen or twenty villages, the total population would have amounted to 4,000 or 5,000.

We have arrived at three estimates. The first, based upon consideration of attrition due to disease and warfare, together with general contemporary statements, gives a range of 3,000-7,500. The second, based upon tribal subdivisions, gives 4,000. The third, derived from village numbers, reaches 4,000-5,000. The average is close to 4,500, a value which seems reasonable under the circumstances.

Before leaving the Massachusetts it will be of interest to estimate the probable density of this tribe. To be sure, density might be regarded as a figment of statistical imagination because, as has been stated, the permanent settlements were concentrated on the coast and a few rivers. However, the hinterland contributed subsistence and was essential to the Indian economy. Hence it must be included in the territory occupied by the tribe as a whole.

The outlines of occupancy have been delineated by many writers, notably Speck (1928b). I have drawn these, of course as an approximation, on the Geological Survey Map of the Eastern United States, scale 1:250,000. I then measured the enclosed area by means of a planimeter, and determined it to be 1,100 square miles. However, a tolerance of at least 100 square miles must be allowed in order to compensate for ignorance of the exact tribal boundaries, if indeed such boundaries existed at all.

If the population is taken as 4,500, the density would have been 4.0 persons per square mile, plus or minus 0.5. The figure is high whem compared to the 0.3 persons per square mile assigned by Mooney (1928) as the aboriginal density throughout the continental United States. On the other hand, it is not unduly great for an area as favorable as the southern New England coast.

### THE WAMPANOAG

The Wampanoag held southeastern Massachusetts as far as Cape Cod. At their northern boundary, which extended from the Pawtucket River to the coast above Plymouth, they met the Massachusetts. On the west they held the land along the east bank of the Pawtucket River and the east shore of Narragansett Bay. On the east they followed the coast as far as the vicinity of Sandwich, on the north shore of Cape Cod. Politically they held sovereignty over some of the Nauset on the Cape and perhaps over the large islands of Martha's Vineyard and Nantucket, but strictly ethnically they seem to have reached their limit at the base of the Cape. If we adhere to Speck's outline (1928b: p. 35) of their holdings, and measure it on the map, the area of their territory is found to be about 1,220 square miles, just a little more than was occupied by the Massachusetts.

Despite the fame which this small tribe has acquired through its dealings with the English during the seventeenth century, and through the tremendous struggle which its warriors made under King Philip, we know relatively little about the aboriginal population. Some estimates, or rather guesses, were made at the time by English observers. The best known of these include the statement attributed to Massasoit, father of King Philip, that he held control over 30 villages, and the sentence of Gookin (1674: p. 168) that the tribe "could raise, as the most reliable and ancient Indians affirm, about three thousand men." That this figure, 3,000 men, may have been standard hyperbole, and intended only to represent a great number, has already been suggested in the case of the Massachusetts. Nevertheless, the population must have been heavy, as is intimated by a few indirect statements of contemporaries.

Some of these express the feelings of the English settlers at Plymouth upon seeing the Indian habitat for the first time. Thus Bradford (1620: p. 117) quotes a letter from Captain Thomas Dermer (dated June 30, 1620) which states that "the *Pocanawkets,* which live to *ye west* of Plimouth . . . are of more strength than all ye savags from thence to Penobscote." William Wood (1634: p. 17) said that "in some places where the Indians dyed of the plague some fourteene yeares agoe, is much underwood, as in the midway between Wessaguscus and Plimouth, because it hath not been burned." The inference is that formerly the population was sufficiently heavy to keep the area clear for planting.

The most circumstantial comment upon the former intense occupancy of the land comes from Mourt, in his *Relation* (1622: pp. 233-235). He describes a journey along the Taunton River, in the heart of the Wampanoag country: "The head of this river is reported to be not far from our place of abode [Plymouth]. Upon it are and have been many towns, it being a good length. The ground is very good on both sides, it being for the most part cleared." Again he says: "Thousands of men have lived there, which died in a great plague not long since, and pity it was to see so many goodly fields and so well seated, without men to dress and manure the same." He writes about the trip down the river: "As we passed along we observed that there were few places by the river but had been inhabited, by reason whereof much ground was clear, save of weeds, which grew higher than our heads." It is quite true that these are all subjective impressions. Nevertheless they create the strong presumption that the Wampanoag were a populous, well-established people.

From these statements, and of course many others, it can be concluded that the Wampanoag, like the Massachusetts, suffered severely from the plague of 1617. There seems to be agreement, however, that the attack was most severe in the northern part of their territory, near the border with the Massachusetts. At Plymouth itself, and at the village of Patuxet, ten or fifteen miles away, it was claimed (Mourt's *Relation,* 1622: p. 276) that all the inhabitants had died. Probably nearly all did die and the few survivors absconded to other settlements. However, the disease attenuated rapidly westward and southward. We hear of no mortality among the Narragansetts to the west or the Nauset to the southeast. The Wampanoag along the shore of Buzzard's Bay and the east shore of Narragansett Bay seem to have been little, if at all, affected. A rough estimate of the damage inflicted by the plague may be made by assuming that one-half of the tribe was within the area of infection, and that in that area the mortality varied from zero to 100 percent. The conclusion would be that one-quarter of the total population was lost.

Evidently attrition due to disease did not cease with the end of the plague in 1618 or 1619, at least in the region of Plymouth. The situation is made very clear by the writings of Governor Edward Winslow (1625: p. 252). In January, 1623, the governor went to Namasket (near Middleboro) to get corn. It was brought partly by Indian women, "but a great sickness arising amongst them, our own men were enforced to fetch home the rest." The following April there was trouble at Mattakeset (near Duxbury). The Indians living there forsook their homes and went to live in the woods and swamps "and so brought manifold diseases amongst themselves, whereof very many are dead. . . . and certainly it is strange to hear how many of late have and still daily die amongst them; neither is there any liklihood it will easily cease; because through fear they set little or no corn, which is the staff of life, and without which they can not long preserve health and strength" (1625: p. 273).

Whether the same conditions existed elsewhere in the territory of the Wampanoag, and how long they persisted in the Plymouth area, cannot be determined from Governor Winslow. However, it is probable that his observations were more or less representative of all southeastern New England, and that the erosion of population due to diseases of various sorts was much more severe than can be explicitly stated from the documents of the time. Such an opinion is reinforced strongly by the appearance of smallpox in 1633, and the appalling susceptibility of all the natives to respiratory ailments and the dysenteries. We have seen how disease substantially annihilated the Massachusetts. Although its effect was not as severe with the Wampanoag, nevertheless this tribe must have suffered drastically during the half-century from 1620-1670.

At the end of this period armed conflict broke out, which within a year or two completed the destruction of the Wampanoag. Although there were numerous survivors, the population was so reduced and the entire tribe so disorganized that no data relating to its condition subsequent to 1675 have any value for the determination of aboriginal population. On the other hand, estimates derived from the immediate pre-war years are of significance.

The Wampanoag, as the backbone of the Indian resistance movement, have always commanded the respect and attention of historians. In the many accounts of King Philip's War there has been a broad attempt to assess the numerical strength of the tribe. The figure which is generally given is 500 warriors (see Hodge, *Handbook,* 1910: Part II, p. 903; Krzywicki, 1934: p. 478; Ellis and Morris, 1906: passim). These fighting men were drawn from all the Wampanoag bands of the mainland, but did not include the Nauset nor the inhabitants of the offshore islands, who may have been related to them ethnically but who did not participate in the war. Prior to 1675 there had been no hostilities and the tribe had enjoyed as stable an existence as was possible for the natives during the seventeenth century. Hence, if we accept the 500 warriors as representing the total military effort, the population must have reached an aggregate of close to 2,000 in 1675.

The attrition due to disease and to economic disruption cannot be estimated exactly, but it must have been severe. The experience of other New England tribes, as well as the scattering accounts, some of which have been mentioned, would suggest at least a 50 percent diminution in the course of the 60 years preceding King Philip's War. We then have to postulate a minimum aboriginal population of 4,000. Mooney's estimate (1928: p. 4) of 2,400 simply will not fit the facts as these are known to us.

A further clue to the population of the Wampanoag lies in the subtribal organization and the known villages. For a careful analysis of the major divisions of the tribe we are indebted to Speck (1928b: pp. 47-77). He lists nine subdivisions, each under a subordinate, local sachem, or chief, and his list is repeated by Swanton (1952: pp. 24-25). In brief, these are, according to the name of the chief:

1. *Massasoit.* He was the head of the entire tribe in 1620 and for several decades thereafter. His personal domain included "a territory called Sowwams on the east side of Narragansett Bay; the western part of Bristol County, Mass.; all of Bristol

County, R.I.; and the eastern part of Providence County, R.I." (Swanton, 1952: p. 24).

2. *Annawon.* He was in Rehoboth.

3. *Weetamoe.* She was in Pocasset, in southeastern Rhode Island, at Taunton, and in adjacent parts of Bristol County, Massachusetts.

4. *Corbitant.* In 1621 he held the region about Swansea.

5. *Tispaquin* and his son. They were southeast of Namasket, and held the adjacent parts of Bristol County, Massachusetts.

6. *Tyask.* He was adjacent to Tispaquin, north of New Bedford.

7. *Totoson.* He held the land between Mattapoisett and Rochester.

8. *Coneconam.* He held the region of Manomet, extending nearly to Sandwich and Woods Hole.

9. *Piowant.* He was on and near the Taunton River.

There was also unoccupied land, chiefly near Plymouth. Speck (1928b: p. 77) explains this condition by saying: "Evidently the neighborhood had been depopulated by the plague . . . as Samoset informed them."

The list is not very satisfactory for demographic purposes, for, as Speck himself suggests, there is considerable overlap in both time and space. Massasoit died a few years after the Massachusetts Bay Colony was founded, and his heirs sold much of the family property to the English. The remainder of the land, together with the authority as tribal chieftain, passed to his son Philip. Two of the sachems mentioned, Corbitant and Coneconam, were subordinates and contemporaries of Massasoit. The others were active after 1650 and fought under Philip in the war of 1675-1676. We have no information concerning the pre-war size of their bands. The result is that we cannot estimate the population of the subtribes separately and add the total.

A clue to size is contained in a statement by Krzywicki (1934: p. 478), who quotes W. Douglas (1760) to the effect that in 1637 the principal settlement at Pokānoket had 300 men, as did also the region of Pocasset. This estimate is supported in general by the claim of Increase Mather, cited by Speck (1928b: p. 68), that Weetamoe, the queen of Pocasset, contributed 300 men to Philip's army in 1675. If, in 1637, these two subtribes, probably the largest among the Wampanoag, contained 600 men, the other divisions, collectively, must have held another 400. The total population would then have reached approximately 3,500 to 4,000. If the decline from 1615 to 1637 due to disease and disturbance amounted to 30 percent of the original population, the latter would have attained the level of 5,000-5,500 souls.

A somewhat different approach is through the number and size of the villages, instead of subtribes. Villages were often synonymous with subtribes; often they were not. Massasoit claimed lordship over 30 villages. At least 2 or 3 of these had been destroyed by the plague; others had been damaged. Thirty, as his pre-plague holding, does not seem excessive.

Hodge, in the *Handbook* (1910: Part II, p. 903), at the end of the article on the Wampanoag, lists 39 villages which he says "probably belonged to the tribe." To these may be added Pokanoket, although it may be the name of the subtribe rather than of a single village, and Patuxet, which existed until 1617. Of the total of 41 villages, 11 are on Nantucket and Martha's Vineyard, and these islands are omitted from consideration here. Two names on the mainland are given which are not mentioned elsewhere by any author known to me, nor is any reference given by Hodge. They may have existed, but there is no evidence for it. After 13 have been deducted, there are left 28. Of these, 13 are noted as having contained at least some praying Indians in the 1670's. The question posed by their inclusion is whether they were villages aboriginally or whether they were founded specifically in order to house the Christian converts. The question, I think, must be answered in favor of their aboriginal existence. The chief evidence for this point of view is negative: none of the villages is stated by Gookin, Bourne, Hawley, or others to have been a new foundation. Such statements would probably have been made if the places were completely new. We may therefore accept 25 as being close to the actual number of permanent settlements of the Wampanoag prior to 1617.

The next problem is that of size. We know that a few of the villages were quite large. Pocasset, Pokanoket, Namasket, and Saconnet must have contained several hundred persons each. Sylvester (1910: Vol. 2, p. 260) mentions that Philip's village, Pocasset, had "above a hundred wigwams . . . covering about 4 acres of ground." At 8 persons per wigwam the population would have been 800. It is likely that none of the villages held less than 100 persons. Most, probably, were in the 200-300 range. A conservative average for all of them would be 200. This means a total population of 5,000.

It is also possible to make indirect use of the villages of the Wampanoag which, after King Philip's War, were inhabited by Christianized Indians. There were not many of these, both because the existing Wampanoag villages had been destroyed in the war and because the Indians were not favorably disposed to the white man's religion. However, there were in 1685, according to Governor Thomas Hinckley (Mass. Hist. Soc., Coll., Series 4, Vol. 5, p. 133), six villages which were wholly Wampanoag, or at least within the territory of the tribe. These were Cooxitt, Cooxisset, Namasket, Namatakeeset, Sekonnet, and Salt Water Pond. The aggregate congregation was 495 adults, all persons above twelve years old. If it be considered that this segment represented 60 percent of the population of these villages, the total would have been 825, or an average of 135-140 people per village — let us say 140.

Although these villages, in 1685, must have represented a good deal of consolidation, for the Indians were badly dispersed by the war, by no means all the surviving Wampanoag were assembled in towns which were actually under white supervision. In order to allow for the aberrant component, the value of 825 may be increased to 1,000. It is highly probable, therefore, that fully 1,000 of the tribe were still living in southeastern Massachusetts a few years after their defeat in 1676.

The principal difficulty with this figure, obtained at such a late date, is that it forces a backward extrapolation. In non-numerical terms it can be truthfully stated that the depletion was extremely severe. Numerically, the loss from 1615 to 1675 has been estimated as 50 percent of the aboriginal value. During the war of 1675-1676 the battle casualties, deaths from starvation and exposure, and the losses through captivity and slavery, must all have accounted for at least half of those alive in 1674, if not for many more. A safe estimate of the survivors would be 40 percent of the 1674 value. Then the population before the struggle would have been 2,500 and the aboriginal level 5,000.

A final method of comparison, although by itself not a very convincing one, is that of area density. The Massachusetts, who lived in a region very similar to the home of the Wampanoag, were calculated to have had a density of 4.0 persons per square mile. The Wampanoag, whose density might have been even higher, lived in an area which by planimeter measurement reached 1,220 square miles. The population might therefore have been 4,880 people.

If the various methods for estimating the aboriginal population of this tribe are now summarized, the result is as follows.

| General consideration of attrition up to 1675 | 4,000 | Estimate based upon villages prior to 1675 | 5,000 |
|---|---|---|---|
| Estimate based upon subtribes | 5,000-5,500 | Estimate based upon villages after 1675 | 5,000 |
| Estimate based upon area density | 4,880 | | |

The methods are consistent in showing a population between 4,000 and 5,500. The figure of 5,000 will therefore be suggested as somewhere near the actual value.

### CAPE COD AND THE ISLANDS

Cape Cod, Martha's Vineyard, and Nantucket in 1620 were inhabited by people who were related to, if not a direct offshoot from, the Wampanoag. Those on Cape Cod were sufficiently distinct to be set apart as the Nauset. The islanders were somewhat different linguistically and politically from the Nauset and more closely resembled the Wampanoag. Exhaustive discussions of the ethnographic problems are presented by Speck (1928b) and by Willoughby (1935). The concern here, however, is not with the ethnic but the demographic aspect of the history of the natives, and for this purpose it will be adequate to consider the aboriginal populations according to the regions they occupied rather than to their tribal affiliation.

In all three areas the Indians had in common the characteristic that they encountered the Europeans early and continuously from the beginning of the sixteenth to the end of the seventeenth century. As a result they not only became familiar with the behavior of the white man but also were exposed repeatedly to his diseases. Strangely enough, they suffered no conspicuous epidemics. Even the plague of 1617 seems to have missed them, if the consensus of contemporary observers can be credited. However, there was no intensive settlement on Cape Cod or the islands much before 1650, and then the occupation was sporadic. A by-product of this state of affairs is the fact that we have little or no firsthand information concerning the condition or population of these Indians. An added factor was the position of neutrality and even favorable attitude toward the English which the Nauset assumed during the troubles of the 1670's. They left the English alone, and the English paid relatively little attention to them. Consequently our knowledge of the early decades is scanty.

At the same time this partial friendliness made possible an activity by the Puritan missionaires which was prevented in other areas by indifference and hostility on the part of the natives. As a result the Indians of Cape Cod, Martha's Vineyard, and Nantucket were almost if not completely christianized by the time of King Philip's War. Since hostilities did not extend to their homeland, the converts did not become apostates, but remained firmly in the Christian church. As a by-product of this relationship there have come down to us several quite complete counts of Christian Indians, counts which can be used to establish beyond much question the population level of these natives at the end of the seventeenth century. This possibility does not exist elsewhere because the proportion of praying Indians among the total was small and indeterminate. From the number of Nauset and islander Indians at this date an attempt may be made to move backwards to the aboriginal value.

The starting point will be Cape Cod. There are three contemporary sources for the population of Christian Indians. The first is a letter by the Reverend Richard Bourne, 1674, reproduced by Gookin, 1674 (Mass. Hist. Soc., Coll., Series 1, Vol. 1, pp. 196-199). The second is a letter by Governor Thomas Hinckley, 1685 (printed in Mass. Hist. Soc., Coll., Series 4, Vol. 5, pp. 132-134). The third is contained among the Stiles Documents in the Mass. Hist. Soc., Coll., Series 1, Vol. 10, pp. 129-134, and is entitled "Account of an Indian Visitation, A.D. 1698. Copied for Dr. Stiles by Rev. Mr. Hawley, missionary at Marshpee, from the printed account published in 1698." The visitation was actually made by the Reverend Mr. Grindal Rawson and the Reverend Mr. Samuel Danforth.

The number of individuals is expressed in various terms, most frequently as persons. However, it is highly probable that this word referred only to adults, or persons of religious responsibility: those over 10-12 years of age. The Reverend Bourne in his letter lists seven villages or groups of villages, under each of which he shows the number of (A) "men and women," and (B) "young men and maids." It is clear that children are not included in these categories. The third class is "of these . . . there is that can read," and the fourth "that can write." Certainly small children would not be expected to read and write.

Governor Hinckley, in presenting his census of Indians in the colony of New Plymouth, reports the number "besides boys and girls under twelve years old, which are supposed to be more than three times as many." Apart from the obvious exaggeration, it is clear that young children are excluded. Rawson and Danforth use various units, such as persons, souls, families, or houses, but state explicitly for Marshpee that there were 57 families "in which are from ten years old and upwards 263 persons." They also refer to the population of Nantucket by saying that "the whole number of adult persons here amount to about 500." Of contrary evidence I have found no case. In no instance is there a statement to the effect that young children and infants are included among the persons or souls who made up the congregation of Indian Christians.

In view of these facts it is legitimate to make an allowance for the very young individuals. With the Wampanoag the fraction twelve years or older was estimated as 60 percent, the fraction below that age at 40 percent of the population. Those who lived on the Cape and the islands could not have been very different.

The Reverend Bourne, in 1674, reported a total of 462 adults on Cape Cod, including Falmouth and as far inland as Wareham. If his figure is assumed to represent 60 percent, the total would be 770. Governor Hinckley, in 1685, listed 944 persons twelve years or older from approximately the same area, but he stated that many of them were not praying Indians. Hence the adjusted total, 1,572, might be expected to exceed that of Bourne. Speck (1928b: p. 122) accepts Hinckley's value of nearly 1,000, but does not adjust for the children.

The visitation of Rawson and Danforth in 1698, as reported by Hawley, shows 348 persons in Sandwich and 263 persons in Marshpee, whereas the population of four other centers is expressed only as families or houses (Rawson, 1698). Some of the houses are said to have held two families. If one-half the houses held two families, the number of families would have amounted to 87. The anonymous author of *A Description and History of Eastham, in the County of Barnstable* (Mass. Hist. Soc., Coll., Series 1, Vol. 8, p. 173, 1802) puts the families at 90, as his "most liberal" estimate. If we use our figure of 87 and if we follow this anonymous writer and call the family number six ("a large allowance for an Indian population"), the total persons will be 522. If the more conservative family number of five is employed, the total is 435. Meanwhile Samuel Treat of Eastham, in a letter of 1693 to Increase Mather, quoted on pp. 171-172 of the same article, stated that the population of the four places was 500. Treat's value is a fair compromise, and represents the entire population, not merely the adults. It is then in order to adjust the figures of Rawson and Danforth for Sandwich and Marshpee. The sum for the two towns is 1,018, which, with the remaining 500, yields 1,518 for Cape Cod.

Here are three counts, covering a span of 25 years: 770 (Bourne), 1,572 (Hinckley), 1,518 (Rawson and Danforth). Even if the two later accounts overestimate, the earlier may be too low. Furthermore, there may have been an influx of refugees after King Philip's War after 1676. It is not feasible to pin down the value too closely. An approximate average will be adequate, an average which may be put at 1,250.

For the island of Martha's Vineyard there exists only one detailed report during the period 1674-1700, that of Rawson and Danforth in 1698. These visitors reported seven places or congregations, with a total of 956 persons. Edgartown is mentioned as having 25 families, or 136 persons, a family number of 5.4. At the same time they ascribed a population of 500 to the island of Nantucket. It is clear that with both islands they were thinking of only those 10-12 years or older. Adjustment for children would show a total of 1,600 on Martha's Vineyard and 830 on Nantucket, or some 2,400 on both islands. There are a few other statements which amplify these figures.

An anonymous author, writing in 1807, published in 1815 *A Description of Duke's County* in the Mass. Hist. Soc., Coll., Series 2, Vol. 3, pp. 38-94. According to him (p. 91): "In 1674 they [the Indians of Martha's Vineyard] were reduced to five hundred families, or about fifteen hundred souls." The family number used here, three, is too low. Other writers use approximately five, and with five the total souls would be 2,500. The same anonymous author (p. 92) again puts the population of Martha's Vineyard at 1,500 in 1674, but that in 1698 at 1,000. Here he evidently follows the direct figures of Rawson and Danforth. However, adjusted for children and with a family number of five, these values become, respectively, 2,500 and 1,500. In any event, it is evident that there must have been a considerable decline between 1674 and 1698.

A modern historian who has made a careful study of the Indians on the islands is L. C. M. Hare (1932). In his life of Thomas Mayhew (p. 44), he quotes Matthew Mayhew, the grandson of Thomas Mayhew: "I have taken the more particular care to make an exact computation that I might vindicate Mr. Cotton Mather from the imputation of our reckoning, when in the life of Mr. Eliot he reckons the number supposed to be on Martha's Vineyard professing the Christian religion, to be sixteen hundred." The time referred to is just prior to King Philip's War, and the persons are those "professing the Christian religion," that is, those of reason. The adjusted number is approximately 2,670. In another place (p. 201) Hare states that in 1674 "it is known that" Mayhew had 1,800 converts. This figure should be adjusted to 3,000, probably for both islands.

The adjusted estimates for Martha's Vineyard in 1670-1675 are all close to 2,500; for 1698 close to 1,500. If Nantucket had 800 in 1698, it no doubt contained fully 1,250 Indians in 1670. There exists, therefore, a fairly stable base line for population estimates in the last third of the seventeenth century.

The first settlement of the islands is usually put at about 1642. That of Cape Cod was a decade earlier. There are a few estimates of the population on the islands at this time, but not for the Cape. Speck (1928b: p. 110) who tends toward conservatism, writes concerning the Martha's Vineyard Indians: "At the time of their conversion by Thomas Mayhew Jr., shortly after 1642, they were ascribed a population of some 1,500." At the other extreme is Zaccheus Macy (1792: p. 157), who says that "At that time [1659] there were near three thousand Indians on Nantucket." Concerning Martha's Vineyard the anonymous author of the *Description of Duke's County* (1807: p. 90) says that "not less than three thousand Indians, it has been generally estimated, were on the island, when it was entered by Mayhew." He repeats this figure for 1642 in his tabulation on p. 92. Hare (1932: p. 44) says: "The native population on the several islands at the time of the first settlement is generally estimated at Martha's Vineyard to have been not less than 3,000 and at Nantucket 1,500. Accounts have set the figure at Nantucket as high as 3,000. Matthew Mayhew . . . estimates the adult persons on both islands at about 3,000. . . ." If the adult population is adjusted for children, the 1642 total for the two islands reaches 5,000, quite close to Hare's figure of 4,500.

The remaining question is twofold. Why did the population decrease so rapidly after 1642, and is the aboriginal population correctly reflected by that in existence in 1642? With respect to the first part of the question the answer is undoubtedly disease. With little or no disturbance due to warfare, the only remaining lethal factor is the battery of European maladies introduced by the English. Some hint of the severity of illness can be gleaned from the statements of observers and historians.

The anonymous author (1807: p. 91) of the *Description of Duke's County* says: "In 1643, and at several other times they were visited by a general disease. This was probably the yellow fever, which was, with the consumption, the disorder of which they commonly died." Hare (1932: p. 92) refers to the same epidemic when he says: "In 1646 a general sickness swept over Martha's Vineyard." Macy's account of Nantucket makes it plain that similar epidemics pursued the Indians of this area as late as the end of the eighteenth century. There is a trace of evidence that the plague of 1617 reached the Nauset of Cape Cod. A line occurs in quotes in the Stiles Papers (Mass. Hist. Soc., Coll., Series 1, Vol. 10, p. 113) at the end of a short document, entitled *An Account of the Potenummecut Indians. Taken by Dr. Stiles on the Spot, June 4, 1792:* "A great plague among the Indians at Potenummecut first before the English came."

Finally there is the interesting story of the encounter of Myles Standish, in 1623, with some Nauset as a result of which there was much illness among the Indians. The incident is described by Governor Winslow in his work *Good News from New England* (1625), as published in the Mass. Hist. Soc., Coll., Series 1, Vol. 8, p. 273. The onslaught of Standish and his men "hath so terrified and amazed them, as in like manner they forsook their houses, running to and fro like men distracted, living in swamps and other desert places, and so brought manifold diseases amongst themselves, whereof many of them are dead, as Canacum, the sachem of Manomet; Aspinet, the sachem of Nauset; and Ianough, sachem of Mattachiest. . . ." The skirmishing may have conduced to exposure and starvation, but disease was surely present.

In view of these items, and others which could be adduced, the second part of the question posed above can be answered in the negative. The aboriginal population is not correctly represented by that found by the English missionaries in 1640 or thereabouts. There had undoubtedly been steady attrition since before the arrival of the permenent settlers. Even though they escaped the full attack by the plague, the Nauset and the islanders had been subject to long and intimate visits by such explorers as Gosnold in 1602, Champlain in 1606, and Smith in 1614. The opportunity for transmission of infection was excellent and must have occurred. We do not, of course, know its degree or severity, but a reasonable estimate can be made. On the islands, if there were 5,000 in 1642, there must have been 6,000 in 1600, say 3,500 on Martha's Vineyard and 2,500 on Nantucket.

On Cape Cod the suggested value of population surviving in 1674 was 1,250. There is no earlier figure available. However, the loss must have been in proportion to that on the islands, for physical and economic conditions were much the same. The estimate for 1674 on Martha's Vineyard and Nantucket was 3,500, and for 1600 it was 6,000. By proportion the population on the Cape in 1600 would have been 2,140, or in round numbers 2,100. The total for all three regions in 1600 would have been 8,100.

In this territory, area-density determinations are of dubious value, for two reasons. The first reason is that so much of Cape Cod and the islands is occupied by water that an adequate estimate of land, and hence living surface, is difficult to obtain by ordinary measurement on a map. The second reason is that in this purely coastal habitat the subsistence regime of the natives was so altered in adapting to marine resources that density is referable to length of shoreline rather than to extent of exposed land. Nevertheless, it is of interest to see what results may be secured by the use of land areas.

With a planimeter and the 1:250,000 map, the gross area of the Nauset on Cape Cod can be determined roughly to be 385 square miles plus or minus 10 or 20 percent. That of Martha's Vineyard similarly comes to 100 square miles, and that of Nantucket to 50 square miles. The estimate for the aboriginal population of the Nauset of Cape Cod was 2,100 souls. Hence the density would be nearly 5.5 persons per square mile. This figure is quite close to the 4 persons found with the Massachusetts, and indicates perhaps a somewhat richer environment. The density on Martha's Vineyard would be 35 and on Nantucket 50 persons per square mile. These values are enormous, and would be entirely impossible were it not for the rich subsistence which the islanders derived from the ocean, particularly fish and shellfish, supplemented by a very active corn cultivation. The problem of subsistence and carrying capacity of the islands has been given exhaustive consideration by archaeologists, ethnographers, and historians, but cannot be treated in full at this point. It will be adequate to state that in view of the ecology of southeastern Massachusetts, there is nothing inherently impossible in the large native populations which lived there, and their very high density in several favorable areas.

# Chapter 4

# RHODE ISLAND, EASTERN CONNECTICUT, CENTRAL AND WESTERN MASSACHUSETTS

## THE NARRAGANSETT

The Narragansett have always been considered the largest single tribe in New England. Their core territory embraced the modern state of Rhode Island west of the main channel of Narragansett Bay and the lower Blackstone River. During the early seventeenth century they conquered or gained control over several small bands along the Connecticut border, the Cowesit, and perhaps some Nipmuck clans to the northwest. At the same time they were in strong competition with the Mohegan. Their intertribal relations and those with the English were complex but pertain to the political history rather than to the demographic background of the tribe.

The Narragansett differ in two important respects from the tribes which have been considered previously. First, owing to their somewhat interior position and the protection offered by the bay, they did not come into direct contact with the white invaders as early or as intensively as the more coastal peoples. As a result they were spared for many years the day-to-day contact which proved so deleterious to the Massachusetts and the Wampanoag. Second, and partially as a consequence of the situation created by the first factor, they did not suffer from disease as severely as their neighbors to the east. It is frequently and explicitly stated that the plague of 1617 did not reach them. Indeed, the first epidemic which they are known to have experienced was that of smallpox in 1633. From that date until 1675 there is no recorded instance of a sweeping sickness, although there is indication from the writings of Roger Williams that they suffered the usual chronic ailments.

These conditions were responsible for the fact that the population loss subsequent to 1620 was not severe in comparison with the devastation which visited other groups. There was some reduction, however, which was not compensated by replacement with refugees from the more eastern tribes. This decline has been noted by historians. Thus Potter (1835: p. 4) says: "The ravages of disease, and the defection of their tributaries, must have greatly diminished their strength, even before the war of 1676." Dorr (1885: p. 219) writes that in 1675 "it seems probable that the tribe had been steadily diminishing, during the thirty years before. The fighting men had slowly wasted away."

The best evidence, however, comes from Roger Williams, who lived close to the Narragansett for many years. In the *Key* (1643) he says (p. 125): "They commonly abound with children, and increase mightily; except the plague fall amongst them, or other lesser sicknesses, and then having no means of recovery, they perish wonderfully." Also (p. 137) he says that when they are sick they visit each other "unlesse it be in infectious diseases, and then all forsake them and flie, that I have often seene a poore House left alone in the wild Woods, all being fled, the living not being able to bury the dead, so terrible is the apprehension of an infectious

disease, that not onely persons, but Houses and the whole Towne takes flight."
There can be little doubt that the Narragansett, in common with all southern New
England tribes, underwent severe attrition because of debilitating chronic ailments.
If we exclude the plague, but include the smallpox of 1633 which killed 700 In-
dians, we may estimate that the Narragansett in 1674 had been reduced to two-
thirds of their original strength.

Estimates of precolonial population have usually been expressed in terms of
warriors. The figure proposed by Williams (1643: p. 125 *et passim;* Trumbull, 1767,
pp. 33, 48), Hubbard (1680: pp. 31-34), and others in the seventeenth century has
centered around 4,000-5,000 men. This number supposes a total population of the
order of 15,000-20,000 people, an excessive estimate. Some of the difficulty was
outlined by Callendar (1739: pp. 128-129), who pointed out that one estimate
might have referred to all the Indians under the political control of the Narragansett
sachem, whereas another estimate might have been restricted to the Narragansett
proper. James Mooney, in the *Handbook* (1910a: Part II, p. 28) rejects most of these
figures rather unceremoniously by saying: "The early estimates as usual greatly exaggerate." In view of the confusion and uncertainty surrounding these guesses it is
probably better to disregard them altogether. In their place we may look at the
esimates of population just prior to King Philip's War, at a time when it was of
critical importance for the English to know how many Indians were opposing them.

A reasonably firm value comes from 1643, when a confrontation occurred between
Miantonomo the Narragansett and Uncas the Mohegan. Bradford (1643: p. 505) says
that the former "came suddenly upon him [Uncas] with 900 or 1,000 men." This
figure has been repeated many times since Bradford, and there is no reason to dis-
credit it. The only remaining question is whether Miantonomo had with him all the
men of military age among the Narragansett. The answer, it appears to me, is that
although he had assembled his front-line army, this did not include all the "men" of
the Narragansett. Hence 1,000 is a subminimal value for this category at this time.

Hubbard, in his *General History of New England* (1680: pp. 31-34), listed the
Narragansett as Indian Society No. 12, and said that before destruction by the
English they had about 2,000 fighting men. This statement was repeated by Benjamin Trumbull (1767: p. 48), who wrote: "The Narragansett sachems were known
at the Commencement of the War to have 2,000 warriors." The discussion by Callendar (1739: pp. 128-129), mentioned previously, gives an estimate of 2,000
warriors made by Thomas and Robert Stanton, who had lived among the tribe
before the war of 1676. On the other hand, Gookin (1674: p. 148), after stating
that in former times the Narragansett could raise 5,000 men, adds that now "all
that people could not make above one thousand able men." Dorr (1885: p. 219),
indirectly supports the latter view when he says that "not more than a thousand
can be shown to have perished in 1675-1676." A greater number, however, is required to justify the statement of James Quanapaug (1675: p. 208) that, after the
heavy loss at the battle of the fort "it is reported, there is seven hundred fighting
men, well armed, left of the Narragansetts." Finally there is the opinion of James
Mooney in the *Handbook* (1910a: Part II, p. 29) that "in 1674 they still num-

bered about 5,000." At a ratio of one to four there would have been some 1,200 warriors.

Secondary evidence for a populous area may be derived from the period 1630-1670. Elisha Potter (1835: p. 16) relates how the ship *Rebecca* visited the Narragansett in 1634 to get corn. The master, Mr. Pierce, said that the country west of the bay was full of Indians. He saw there about 1,000 men, women, and children, and yet many were away hunting. There is also the well-known statement by Roger Williams (1643) that a traveler would see a dozen Indian towns in the space of twenty miles, although he did not specify where this stretch was located.

The preponderance of opinion appears to favor a figure closer to 2,000 than to 1,000 warriors at the beginning of King Philip's War, particularly since this number may include the allied or neutral tribes under control of the Narragansett, such as the Cowesit, the Eastern Niantic, and Pumham's band. Because the exact figure cannot be determined, the conservative estimate of Mooney may be used, 1,250 men. The total population can then be taken as 5,000.

When we now apply the factor of two-thirds in order to allow for the decline caused by disease during the more than half-century from 1620 to 1675, we get an aboriginal population of 7,500. If this value seems great, it may be remembered that there are implied only 2,000 warriors, which is not more than half the number claimed by Williams, Hubbard, and other contemporary observers.

Data concerning permanent villages, which become so useful with other tribes, are limited with the Narragansett. In Hodge's *Handbook* (1910: Part II, p. 29) only eight Narragansett and Niantic villages are listed, an incredibly small number for such a large tribe. They are Charlestown, Chaubatick, Maushapogue, Mittaubscut, Narragansett, Niantic, Pauchauquet, and Shawomet. They may be considered in detail:

> *Charlestown.* This is a township in Washington County, Rhode Island, where, in 1907, a few Narrangansett were still living. It may have been a village in colonial times.
>
> *Chaubatick.* This was a Narragansett village near Providence. Roger Williams called it a "town."
>
> *Maushapogue.* This was a village near Providence. No details concerning it are known.
>
> *Mittaubscut.* This Narragansett village was seven miles up the Pawtuxet River. Williams (Mass. Hist. Soc., Coll., Series 3, Vol. 1, p. 71, 1825) says it contained 20 houses with 20 men plus women and children. The total population would have been near 100.
>
> *Narragansett.* This was the principal village and the home of the head chief. It may have been the seat of the Saunck Squaw, otherwise known as Magnus, or Matanuk. In any event there was a large village near Kingston, Rhode Island. It is described by Ellis and Morris (1906: pp. 145-146) as "undoubtedly the deserted village destroyed by the army on the 14th December, 1675." Here the English burnt "over one hundred and fifty wigwams." Ellis and Morris (p. 147, n. 1) quote Sidney S. Rider as saying that "the Queen's Fort was the spot

around which lay the great 'town' of the Narragansetts in 1675." A village of 150 or more wigwams would have contained at least 750 people, and more likely close to 1,000.

*Niantic.* This is said by Hodge (1910: Part II, p. 69) to have been the chief village of the Niantic, near Niantic, Connecticut. If that was its location it probably belonged to the Western Niantic, who were not closely associated with the Narragansett.

*Pauchauquet.* This place is mentioned only as probably a Narragansett village in western Rhode Island.

*Shawomet.* This was a Narragansett village near Warwick, Rhode Island, and was the home of the prominent sachem Pumham. Winthrop, in his *Journal* for the year 1643 (Vol. 1, p. 125), says that Pumham, sachem of Shawomet, had 200-300 men, jointly with Saconococo, sachem of Pawtuxet, but that these chiefs were subordinate to Miantonomo. The number of men indicated would mean a population of at least 1,000, but these might have been dispersed among two or three settlements. In any event the village, or perhaps the subtribe, must have amounted to several hundred souls. This idea is supported by the fact that on Dec. 27, 1675, the English destroyed 100 wigwams in Pumham's village.

To the above list should be added the following:

*Cowesit.* This was a village, or small tribe, on the west bank of the Blackstone River, which was absorbed by the Narragansett in the 1630's.

*Weckapaug.* This was the principal village of the Eastern Niantic under Ninigret. This tribe did not join Philip in his war on the English, but it was considered subject to the Narragansett. The village was located near Charlestown, Rhode Island, and may be identical with the village listed under that name.

Of the above ten villages, or subtribes, two, Charlestown and Pauchauquet, may be excluded as of dubious existence. One, Niantic, may be excluded as not being Narragansett. Three, Chaubatick, Maushapogue, and Mittaubscut may be allowed as small places, with perhaps 100 persons each. The Cowesit were a small tribe with possibly 250 souls. The Eastern Niantic under Ninigret may be allowed a population of 500. The other two villages, Narragansett and Shawomet, were large, with probably fully 1,000 persons each. The total, just before Philip's War, is 3,250. This figure is much smaller than the 5,000 which was derived from contemporary estimates. The difference is, however, simply accounted for by the fact that the village list is defective. It by no means includes all the settlements of the Narragansett in the period 1670-1674. If allowance is made for those places which are missing, the correspondence between the two methods will become reasonably clear.

With regard to aboriginal population the village list tells us little if anything. We know nothing about the number, location, and size of the villages prior to the intervention of the English in the affairs of the Narragansett. We do know that there was considerable shifting of settlements and realignment of bands as a result of the Pequot War (1637) and other disturbances to the westward. We also know that the Narragansett were prone to shift their homes with the seasons and for other reasons (see Bushnell, 1919: pp. 20-21). Therefore we can say merely that the village list given here tends to support only the estimate of population in 1674. It is still necessary to rely upon the reduction ascribed to disease in order to arrive at the possible aboriginal level.

The population density of the Narragansett can be calculated approximately. The area of Rhode Island to the west of the bay and the Blackstone River is about 900 square miles. It is proper to add another 100 square miles in order to allow for islands in the bay and possible extensions of Narragansett control into Massachusetts and Connecticut. The total land held, therefore, is not far from 1,000 square miles. An aboriginal population of 7,500 would show a density of 7.5 persons per square mile. This figure is somewhat greater than is derived for the tribes in southeastern Massachusetts, but is warranted in view of the extensive coastal habitat.

In conjunction with the Narragansett it is instructive to consider the natives of Block Island, south of the Rhode Island coast. The main facts of their habitation are incontrovertible. These people had been visited by numerous explorers and traders, but maintained their independent status until the settlement of the mainland near them. In 1633 they were invaded by the English, under Captain John Underhill. He has left a perfectly veracious account of the affair (Mass. Hist. Soc., Coll., Series 3, Vol. 6, pp. 6-7) written in 1638, and it has also been described by Winthrop in his *Journal* (1636, pp. 187-188). The English were met by 50-60 "able fighting men," whom they routed. There were two villages, with a total of 60 wigwams, "some large and fair," and some 200 acres of corn. According to the number of warriors there might have been 250 people in all. On the other hand, 60 wigwams might have contained close to 400. A fair compromise is 300 persons, 150 in each village.

Several points of interest are raised by the situation on Block Island. It is clear that this small island, when Underhill landed in 1633, was almost, if not quite, in the aboriginal state. There is no indication of serious depletion due to disease, in spite of the island's exposed position. The support basis was unusually copious — 200 acres of corn for 300 people, plus unlimited marine food. The area of land surface was small, not more than 10 square miles. The density would therefore have reached 30 persons per square mile, and perhaps more. This figure is four times that postulated for the Narragansett, and is of the same order as that found on Martha's Vineyard. The 300 Indians ascribed to Block Island may be added for convenience to the total of the Narragansett, making the final estimate 7,800 in precolonial times.

### THE MOHEGAN AND THE PEQUOT

If one attempts to estimate the initial population of these two tribes he is immediately forced to consider their political history during the early years of the seventeenth century. Probably not long before the arrival of the English, the Algonkian people who constituted the future Mohegan and Pequot entered eastern Connecticut, displaced the occupants, and settled the entire area from the Connecticut River to the Rhode Island line in the southeastern part of the state. In 1630 the combined people, who were then considered Pequot, lived under the rule of the sachem Sassacus, who was succeeded by Uncas. The latter became known as the chief of the Mohegans. Speck (1928a: p. 207) describes the evolution clearly:

First appearing as an organized tribe under the celebrated leader Uncas, the Mohegan gradually assumed the prominence of a great political factor in southern New England. Although the name Marhicans (Mohegan) is given a place on a map of the region dating from 1614, . . . their ancestry was chiefly Pequot. . . . How they gradually developed into a separate nationality . . . is generally well known.

In effect, this means that in the years prior to 1620 the tribe was actually the Pequot, and it is the number of these people which would determine the aboriginal population, not the number of Mohegans who inhabited the area subsequent to 1640. The course of the history of the two tribes is further complicated by the Pequot War of 1637, during which the majority of the combined group, under the name of Pequots, was destroyed or dispersed by the English. The survivors were scattered, and many of them went to live with the other component, the Mohegans under Uncas. As a result, the number of Mohegans, as they were now called, probably underwent an increase.

Estimates of population have generally been based upon the number of warriors who participated in the Pequot War, and the size of the army of Uncas. Towns and villages cannot be used because these settlements were moved in space or altered in time by the changing fortunes of the Indians. There are no archaeological data, and density figures are of little value because the area occupied by the Pequot-Mohegan was confined within very unstable limits. The shifts in territory are well illustrated by the map supplied in the paper by Speck (1928a: pl. 20).

The figure 3,000 has been associated with the early Pequot, or the combined tribe. Thus Orr (1897: p. viii) says: "Their total strength at that time is estimated to have been about 3,000." Speck (1928a: p. 213) says: "About 3,000 before the Pequot War is the estimate given by early writers." Mooney in the *Handbook* (1910b: Part II, p. 230) says: "At the period of their greatest strength the Pequot probably numbered at least 3,000 souls, but have been estimated much higher." In his later paper (1928: p. 4) he lists the combined Pequot and Mohegan as having 2,800 persons.

This value is consistent with the figure 700 which has frequently been mentioned as the number of warriors, or "men." An extensive discussion of this estimate was contributed by De Forest (1853: pp. 58ff). He thought that 700 was too large a number and that it should be reduced to 500-600. His reasons were based upon considerations of (a) density, and (b) casualties at the battle of the Mystic River fort. With respect to density he estimated the territory of the Pequot as 500 square miles. He then says that 700 warriors would mean a population of 3,500, or 7 persons per square mile. This, he thought, was too high. However, with the usual, and quite liberal factor of four persons per warrior, the total is 2,800 and the density is 5.6 persons per square mile. This value is close to that found for other nearby mainland tribes, and does not indicate an overestimate of number of men.

It should also be possible to calculate the number of warriors present before the war by adding the survivors to those who died in the struggle. In the Mystic fort some 600 Indians probably perished (Cook, 1973b), including the approximately 150 men who came as reinforcements from the upper fort. Of these fully 200 must have been fighting men, although the majority of the casualties were non-combatants. After this battle there was skirmishing in which the Indians suffered further. Thus Underhill (1638: p. 27) describes a fight in which 100 Pequots are said to have been killed or wounded. Also 200-300 fugitives were trapped in a swamp near Fairfield, Connecticut. All the women and children were captured, but 40-60 warriors escaped, with the death of a few. A loss of 100 men is reasonable to allocate to this sporadic fighting, which lasted throughout the winter of 1637-1638. The total of the warriors killed would therefore reach close to 300.

After the fighting the Pequots were widely scattered. Many escaped to southwestern Connecticut and Long Island. A few even reached the Delaware on the Hudson. Sassacus with some 80 men went to the Mohawks to seek help (Roger Williams, 1637, Letter to Winthrop), but as far as is known they were either killed or absorbed by the Iroquois. Many others were handed over to local tribes, particularly the Mohegan, who now became predominantly Pequot ethnically. Mooney (*Handbook,* 1910b: Part II, p. 230), whose figures are repeated by Speck (1928a: p. 213), says that 350 men were included among those who sought refuge in New Haven and on Long Island, and 200 were sent to local tribes. If we accept these figures, and reckon another 100 as having escaped clear of New England, the total is 650 men. With the 300 who probably perished in battle, the aggregate is 950 warriors. This value may be too high, but it supports the figure of 700, which was disputed by De Forest (1853: p. 58). The combined tribes in 1637 must have contained at least 3,000 people.

This estimate is supported by subsequent data. In 1643 at the famous meeting of Miantonomo the Narragansett and Uncas the Mohegan, mentioned above (p. 00), Miantonomo was said to have been accompanied by 900-1,000 warriors, but Uncas had "not half so many" (Hubbard, 1680: p. 457). Thus Uncas might have had 450 warriors and his tribe would have reached 1,800. Holmes (1804: p. 77) thought the total was 1,500. Mooney (1907: Part I, p. 926) says that in the same year (1643) the Mohegan were estimated at 2,000-2,500, but this included the Pequot living with them. We may take 2,200 for the combination.

Mooney makes the statement, which is repeated by Speck, that the Pequots, having been gathered upon two reservations at Ledyard and Groton, had a population of 1,500 in 1674. There were at this time also many Mohegan, for their total in 1704 was estimated by De Forest to be 750. The value for the Pequot may be exaggerated, for the population of the joint Pequot-Mohegan cannot well have exceeded 1,500 by the year 1700.

The resistance of these tribes to the forces which operated upon them as the result of settlement by whites, as well as the recovery of the Pequot from the great blow dealt them in 1637, excites admiration. It also is evidence that the total number alive in, say, 1635, was fully as great as has been indicated by early estimates, and by the numbers recorded. If, prior to 1637, there was relatively little contact with Europeans, no disturbance due to warfare, and no severe epidemics, it is probable that the number estimated at the beginning of the Pequot War was nearly the pre-contact value. If this number is set with some assurance at 3,000, the aboriginal level could not have exceeded 3,500 souls.

### THE NIPMUCK AND THE CONNECTICUT VALLEY BANDS OF MASSACHUSETTS

The interior of Massachusetts was occupied by an agglomeration of more or less autonomous bands, most of which were known collectively as the Nipmuck. Whatever may have been their prior experience, at the time they became known to the invading white men they constituted a loosely coordinated confederacy, not a homogeneous, unified tribe such as the Narragansett, Pequot, or Mohegan. For this reason it is necessary to examine separately the individual components rather than attempt to assess the strength of the "tribe" as a whole.

The boundaries which we set for this people, in order to estimate their population, are dictated by geographical as opposed to ethnic considerations. The primary deviation from the conventional pattern is seen in the inclusion of the bands who lived in that portion of the Connecticut Valley which lies in Massachusetts. These groups may or may not have been Nipmuck in the strict sense, but they bordered on this tribe and for the purpose of demographic study they are best treated as part of it.

An instructive picture of the Indian settlements is given on the map published by Bullen (1941), entitled "Distribution of 1,013 Indian Sites." Although the actual number of dots on Bullen's map is no guide, their placement is. Clearly the Indian habitations followed the small streams which take their origin in the highlands of central Massachusetts, and were also concentrated in the broad, flat Connecticut Valley. These streams include the headwaters of the Nashua, Blackstone, and Quinebaug rivers, together with the entire Chicopee River system. To these we may add the lower few miles of the Westfield and Deerfield rivers. The Miller's River system should also be mentioned, for it was inhabited, despite the paucity of sites shown on Bullen's map.

The most ambitious recent attempt to delineate the boundaries of the Nipmuck is that of Gahan (1941). He starts his circuit at Littleton, Massachusetts, with the Nashoba and runs his line through Concord, Natick, Cochituate, Medway, and Bellingham to the Mill River at Blackstone. He thus includes territory which here has been considered as pertaining to the Pennacook (Littleton) and the Massachusetts (Natick, Cochituate). In the north he puts the boundary along Miller's River east to Athol and from there through Lunenburg back to Littleton. In the south, Gahan cuts across northwestern Rhode Island into Connecticut and pursues a westerly trend to Enfield. Here he turns north "along the valley of the Connecticut" to Northfield. I would be more specific and cross the river west of Enfield. Thence I would follow north along the front range of the Berkshire Hills to Northfield. The result would be to include all the Connecticut Valley tribes, whether or not they were truly Nipmuck.

### The Northeastern Sector

This is the territory of the Nashua and the Wachusett. It extends from Littleton, Concord, and Sudbury, Massachusetts, westward to Sterling and Mt. Wachusett. The two subtribes, which were considered to have had about 700 members, were allocated to the Pennacook (see p. 00). Hence they will not be considered as Nipmuck.

### The Southeastern Sector

Here we circumscribe an area bounded on the north by Worcester, Marlboro, and Framingham, and on the east and southeast by Medway, Bellingham, and Blackstone. On the west and southwest the line follows roughly the course of the Blackstone River from the Rhode Island border to Worcester. There are no subtribes or divisions here to which any name but Nipmuck has been given. Indeed, we know nothing of the area save what has been preserved in the records of Gookin, who, with John Eliot, proselyted actively among these natives. In Gookin's work, published by the Massachusetts Historical Society in 1792, and probably written in 1674, he lists in detail 14 villages which contained Christian Indians.

Some of these towns he calls "old" and some "new." Of the "old" towns, four — Natick, Punkapog, Wamesit, and Nashoba — lie outside the region here concerned. Hassanamesit at Groton, Okommakamesit at Marlboro, and Magunkaquog at Hopkinton, may be considered Nipmuck rather than Pennacook or Massachusett. With respect to the "new" praying towns Gookin remarks (1674: p. 189) ". . . for distinction sake we call the new praying towns in the Nipmuck country." Of them, two — Pakachoog at Worcester (Millbury, according to Swanton, 1952: pp. 22-23) and Waeuntug or Wacuntug at Uxbridge — may be allocated to this sector. In these five places in 1674 there were 315 "souls yielding obediance to the gospel" (1674: p. 195). We have previously determined that persons over 12 years of age are meant, and that these constituted 60 percent of the population. The total for the five villages would then have been 525.

The attrition of population in this area during the 50 years from 1620-1670 perhaps was not as great as that among the more coastal tribes. On the other hand, it is probable that the plague reached inland a good many miles and that the subsequent exposure to settlers and their diseases was considerable. A reduction of one-third from the aboriginal number may be allowed, and that value may be set at 790, or in round numbers 800.

### The Wabaquasset and the Quinnebaug

These two subtribes inhabited the headwaters of the Quinnebaug River in northeastern Connecticut and southern Massachusetts. Gahan (1941) thinks that they also extended into northwestern Rhode Island. Their territory, therefore, lay to the west and southwest of the sectors described above.

The Wabaquasset are said by Hodge (1910: Part II, p. 885) to have been a tribe or band, with a village south of Woodstock, Connecticut. Swanton (1952: p. 23) mentions the village as being Nipmuck, although he adds that it was "sometimes regarded as an independent tribe." The existence of at least the village is consequently established, with perhaps 200 inhabitants.

The Quinnebaug were certainly a larger group. Swanton (1952: pp. 22-23), whose list is reasonably full, mentions no less than eight villages which belonged to the Nipmuck in northeastern Connecticut, apart from Wabaquasset. In addition he includes one near Dudley, Massachusetts, and another at Oxford, Massachusetts. The total number of villages in the upper Quinnebaug basin is ten, which, if they were simultaneously occupied and if each contained 100 inhabitants, would imply an aggregate of 1,000 people.

Further evidence comes from Gookin (1674: p. 195), who reports very active missionizing in this area. He lists five "new" praying towns: Manchoge at Oxford, Chabanakongkomum at Dudley, and Maanexit, Quantisset, and Wabquisset at or near Woodstock. Together they had 455 adults, or 760 people. Furthermore, it must be remembered that the missionaries by no means converted all these Indians. Many still remained in heathendom. Moreover, the depletion due to disease during the period before King Philip's War, although it may have been relatively light, was defintely present. If these factors are given appropriate weight, the conclusion must be that the aboriginal population was little less than 1,000. When the Wabaquasset are added, the total reaches fully 1,200.

## The Quaboag

The subtribe had its home in the rolling hill and lake country along the Quaboag and Ware rivers west of Worcester and north of Southbridge. It was never missionized nor, indeed, was it penetrated to any great extent before King Philip's War. Hence our knowledge of it is derived mainly from protohistoric and archaeological evidence.

One quite full account is that found in a paper by Phelps (1948), who republished excerpts from the "History of North Brookfield" by Josiah H. Temple, 1887. No quotation marks or page references appear in the text. Phelps, or rather Temple, mentions seven villages or other settlements: (1) Wekaboag, "the largest of those Quaboag villages," was on Wekaboag Pond in West Brookfield. (2) "The other permanent village," Quobagud, was on Quaboag Pond in East Brookfield. (3) Ashquoach, "an important Quaboag village, often named in the early records," was in Brimfield. It had a fort and was occupied until 1675. (4) Another Ashquoach was named in a deed of 1665 as being on Quaboag Pond. (5) Quassuck was a "small cluster of Indian wigwams" at Sturbridge. (6) Putikookuppog was a "large village of Quaboags" near the present line between Sturbridge and Brimfield. (7) An "Indian settlement" existed in the northeast part of Warren. The settlement may have been established after the war of 1675. A lodge was still standing in 1746. "Besides these clearly marked village sites" there were numerous other small temporary village or camp sites which are not listed.

If we discard site no. 7 as of doubtful origin, there are six reasonably well authenticated Quaboag settlements. Quassuck (no. 5) is stated to have been a "small cluster" of wigwams. The rest are called "large" or "important," with Wekaboag the largest. There may have been 200 persons in this village, and 100 in each of four others. The smallest may have held 50. The sum is 650, but to account for scattered families another 50 may be added. The total, then, would be 700.

In 1675, during the height of King Philip's War, the inhabitants of all these

villages departed from their homes and reconstituted their settlements on the
Menemesek, or Ware, River, at New Braintree. Shortly thereafter, in November,
1675, the area was visited by James Quanapaug, whose statement is published in the
Massachusetts Historical Society Collections, Series 1, Vol 6, pp. 205-208, 1800.
He found the Quaboag established in three villages, three miles apart, with 300 warriors plus women and children. Some depletion may have occurred as the result of
the exigencies of war, and therefore we shall use a factor of three instead of four.
The total would have been 900 souls. Attrition must have reduced the population to
some extent between 1620 and 1670, but, in the reverse sense, some of the people
seen by Quanapaug in 1675 may have come from other tribes.

The two estimates, one from field observation, the other from a documentary
source, are very close. The population of the Quaboag subtribe may therefore be
set at the median, or 800 people.

## Miller's River

Along this river, between Turner's Falls and Fitchburg, there must have lived
Indians, and yet I can find no firm record of any bands or villages. It is true that
Bullen (1941) shows a few sites there on his distribution map, and that Gahan
(1941) lists the Pequeags, "questionably Nipmuck," as "of Miller's River." However, Hodge does not mention this name, nor does Swanton (1952) nor any other
source available to me. It might be possible to make a guess at the number of
Indians who inhabited this valley, but in view of the total lack of concrete evidence
it is preferable to leave it blank.

## The Pocumtuc

The name Pocumtuc has been applied to a tribe or band living at or near Deerfield, and also to the entire chain of small subtribes which extended from
northern Connecticut up the Connecticut River to the Vermont and New Hampshire border. Hodge, in the *Handbook* (1910: Part II, p. 170), places the Agawam
at Springfield, the Nonotuc at Northampton, the Norwottuc at South Hadley,
the Pocumtuc proper at Deerfield, the Squawkeag at Northfield, and the Woronoke
at Westfield. Hoyt (1824: p. 91) gives much the same list but says that they were
all generally called Pocumtucks. Judd (1905: p. 115) mentions the Agawams,
Woronokes, Norwottucks, and Pocumtucs. Swanton (1952: pp. 23-24), under the
main heading Pocumtuc, places the Agawam, Nonotuc, Pocumtuc and Squawkeag.
Wright (1949: p. 18) specifically names the Nonotuc at Northampton and the
Woronoco at Westfield, together with the Shipmuck at Chicopee Falls.

It is widely held that these groups were a heterogeneous residue of Nipmuck
plus perhaps Mohegan, Pennacook, and other stocks which had been disturbed by
the Mohegan-Pequot invasion and by Mohawk raids in the comparatively recent
past. The ethnic difficulties can be avoided, however, if we consider the various
divisions separately as they were first encountered by the white man.

With respect to Connecticut, Gahan (1941) runs the Nipmuck boundary
"westerly from Killingly through Danielsonville, Ashford, Shenapsic Lake and

Enfield," but he mentions no villages or subtribes in this area. Swanton (1952: p. 24) lists three villages under the Pocumtuc: Mayawang near West Suffield, and Nameroke and Scitico at or near Enfield. He cites no reference for the inclusion of these, and they are not to be found in the *Handbook* (1910). Nevertheless it is highly probable that they, or their equivalent, existed in the early seventeenth century. They may not have been large, and to ascribe 200 souls to all of them would be quite adequate.

The Agawam, with their principal and perhaps only village on Long Hill in Springfield, are well known. They seem to have been relatively numerous, and are called a subtribe by Ellis and Morris (1906: p. 18). In King Philip's War there were 100 Indians engaged in the fighting around Springfield, mostly Agawam. If the tribe had nearly 100 warriors in 1675, the total population must have reached at least 300. Thirty-five years earlier John Underhill (1638: p. 63) in his description of the Connecticut River speaks of the "upper plantations," which were at Windsor, Connecticut. He then says: "Twelve miles above this plantation is situated a place called Aguawam, no way inferior to the fore named places." Although no numbers are specified, a strong group is implied, one of at least 300 souls.

The Shipmuck at Chicopee Falls, Massachusetts, are mentioned only by Wright (1949: p. 18) and can have consisted of no more than a village. A safe estimate of their strength is 100 persons. The Nonotuc, who had a village on a bluff near Northampton, are said by Ellis and Morris (1906: p. 18) to have been a subtribe of the Nipmuck, but others place them in the Pocumtuc. They may be estimated as having 200 persons. Another similar group was the Norwottuc, who lived in the region of Hadley. They had been attacked by the Mohegan in 1656, and they participated in King Philip's War. After this struggle they dispersed. They probably did not number more than 200.

The Pocumtuc proper had their principal village at Deerfield, near which they built a fort. This was destroyed by the Mohawks in 1666, and the subtribe suffered severely. This event was described by John Winthrop, Jr., in a letter of 1664 to Roger Williams (Mass. Hist. Soc., Coll., Series 4, Vol. 6, p. 531): "they are all fled from Pocumtuck and Squakeage and Woruntuck and it seames some of them to your parts but there are 2 forts of them neere Springfield." The attacks of the Mohawks may have been one factor which, according to Ellis and Morris, caused them to waste away prior to King Philip's War, although these authors ascribe the decline to the bad influence of the whites. Nevertheless, one story has it that in the battles around Deerfield an English soldier came upon 60 Pocumtuc warriors. This number implies a substantial residue of population. Probably 300 souls will be adequate.

The Squawkeag were a tribe or band which occupied considerable territory on the Connecticut River from Greenfield to above the New Hampshire line. They are spoken of by Ellis and Morris (1906: p. 18) as a subtribe of the Nipmuck, and their ethnic affiliation has been examined in detail by Day (1965). This investigator has decided through a study of linguistics that the Squawkeag were the "Sokoki" to whom many references were made by early writers and who were confused with the Pennacook (or Abnaki) group on the Saco River. He believes that the Squawkeag may have extended many miles up the Connecticut, but the evidence is not strong. However, Price (1967: p. 8) refers to the "ancient Squawkeag village which was located at what is now, Hinsdale". This village in New Hampshire must have been in addition to that one which was located at Northfield, Massachusetts (Hodge, 1910: Part II, p. 630) and which must have contained at least 300 souls. The village at Hinsdale, together with that at Northfield, plus smaller and unknown settlements, may have brought the band up to the 500 level.

The Waranoke, or Woronoke, were located on the river just west of Westfield, Massachusetts. They were harassed by the Mohawks, but enough of them survived to participate in King Philip's War. No estimate of the population exists, but it must originally have amounted to at least 100.

CONCLUSION

The rough estimates based upon individual bands or subtribes which inhabited the Connecticut Valley now appear as follows. The Nipmuck in Connecticut had 200; the Agawam, 300; the Shipmuck, 100; the Nonotuck, 200; the Norwottuc, 200; the Pocumtuc proper, 300; the Squawkeag, 500; the Waranoke, 100. The total is 1,900, a value which may be taken to apply in the decade just prior to the war of 1675-1676. The raids of the Mohawk, together with the debilitation ensuing upon contact with the white man, were undoubtedly effective in causing severe attrition. However, the erosion cannot have been as lethal as it was in the Boston-Plymouth area. We therefore set the aboriginal number at approximately 2,500.

For the entire region covered by the Nipmuck and the Connecticut Valley bands, we have the following separate estimates: for the northeastern sector (Nashua and Wachusett), 700; for the southeastern sector, 800; for the Wabaquasset and the Quinnebaug, 1,200; for the Quaboag, 800; for the Pocumtuc in the extended sense, 2,500. If the northeastern sector is excluded, the total for the remainder is 5,300.

There are a few data which may be employed to check on this estimate, and which are applicable to substantial blocks of territory. Judd (1905: p. 115) says that the Agawam, Waranoke, Norwottuc, and Pocumtuck proper had a population of 1,000-1,100 "when most numerous." Their numbers, however, did not exceed 800 in 1675. We have estimated 900 for these groups in 1674, and about 1,200 aboriginally.

Ellis and Morris (1906: p. 18) ascribe a total of 1,000 warriors to the entire Nipmuck nation in King Philip's War. This figure requires a population of 4,000. If we allow a reduction of one-third from 1620 to 1674, the aboriginal value would be close to 6,000. Our estimated aboriginal total for all the Nipmuck and Valley groups, including the Nashua and Wachusett is 6,000. If these two subtribes, which have been considered as Pennacook, are omitted, the total is 5,300.

An interesting calculation has been provided by Wright (1949: pp. 18-19). This author examined the land sales made by the Indians to William Pynchon and other settlers in the Springfield region. He then computed the area of land sold by each individual and determined that each person who signed a deed disposed of 1 - 1-1/2 square miles. Hence, if a considerable number of such sales were averaged, it could be calculated that the density of persons in a position to sign these deeds was one for each 1 - 1-1/2 square miles. Wright thought that this finding indicated a small population. However, the signatories to deeds were heads of families, and we must apply a factor of five to get the entire population. Then we find 5 persons to each 1 - 1-1/4 square mile, or approximately 4 per single square mile.

The Connecticut Valley as a whole is indeterminate in precise area. Nevertheless, we may make a reasonably close estimate by taking the area between the front ranges of hills to east and west. If this territory is roughly outlined on the map, and the Mt. Tom-Mt. Holyoke range is deleted, the result is 450 square miles, plus or minus 50 square miles, from Hinsdale, New Hampshire, to Enfield, Connecticut. Then, if we apply the Wright-Pynchon density factor, we get a population of 1,800 souls. The date here is past the midmark of the seventeenth century. Hence the result may be compared with the 1,900 previously estimated for the same region.

These findings are internally consistent within the margin of error to be expected for such estimates. The aboriginal population of central and west central Massachusetts will be set at 5,300 Indians.

Chapter 5

# WESTERN CONNECTICUT AND THE LOWER HUDSON VALLEY: THE WAPPINGER CONFEDERACY

The Wappinger Confederacy consisted of a group of tribes which extended from Poughkeepsie to Manhattan on the Hudson River and thence eastward to the Connecticut. The component tribes were some eight or ten in number and were themselves split into subtribes some of which may have been single villages. The earliest names were applied by the Dutch at a time when knowledge of Indian ethnic organization was very rudimentary. A later nomenclature was employed by the English, who saw the Indians from a different geographical and political standpoint. The result has been considerable confusion in the definition of the native groups, which even now has not been clarified.

For the purpose of examining population, it is preferable to bypass terminology as far as is practicable, and also to avoid controversy relative to intratribal affiliation. Therefore a purely empirical system has been adopted based upon geographical criteria. At the same time a restricted number of historical authorities are utilized in order to simplify the organization of knowledge, even at the risk of omitting mention of writers who, on other grounds, would require consideration. The primary sources for delineation of Indian groups will be the *Handbook of American Indians,* edited by Hodge (1907 and 1910), Ruttenber's *History of the Indian Tribes of Hudson's River* (1872), and Swanton's *Indian Tribes of North America* (1952). For certain parts of New York State reliance has also been placed upon Robert Bolton's *History . . . of the County of Westchester* (1881).

Hodge (1910: Part II, p. 913) divides the Wappinger into nine tribes: Wappinger proper, Manhattan, Weckquaesgeek, Sint-sink, Kitchawanc, Tankiteke, Nochpeem, Siwanoy, and Mattabesec. The last tribe covered most of western Connecticut; the ohters were in New York. Ruttenber (1872: p. 77) lists nine chieftaincies: Wappingers, Manhattans (or Reckgawawancks), Weckquaesgeeks, Sint-sinks, Kitchawongs, Tankitekes, Nochpeems, Siwanoys, and Sequins (Mattabesec). This is essentially the same list that was accepted by Hodge (1910).

More recently two lists have been compiled by Swanton (1952: pp. 44-48). The first is entitled "subdivisions or 'sachemships,' " the second "villages." The village list, which contains 68 names, gives the location of each place. It is regrettable that Swanton could not have included his sources of information, for this list cannot be reconciled with any other. The first list gives as "sachemships" (or "sachemdoms"): Wappinger proper, Wechquaesgeek, Sintskink, Kitchawank, Tankiteke, Nochpeem, and Siwanoy. The Manhattan are listed under the Delaware (see Swanton, 1952: pp. 33 and 49). The Mattabesec are shown as one of the component subdivisions of the Wangunk sachemdom.

The Mattabesec, according to Ruttenber and to Hodge, are to be considered a tribal unit subordinate to the Wappinger Confederacy. Speck (1928a: pl. 20) on his map shows western Connecticut to be the home of the "Mattabesec or Wappinger Confederacy," with several subdivisions which differ from those of Hodge and of Ruttenber. Swanton more or less follows Speck's organization, but there are several differences.

For the subtribes, or bands, of the Mattabesec, there are listed by Ruttenber 8 names, by Hodge 11 names, and by Swanton 10 names. Many of these are duplicated. Some are spelling variants; some are called villages by Swanton. If the duplications are eliminated, the residue consists of 15 subtribes: Hammonasset, Paugusset, Uncowa, Wepawaug, Quinnipiack, Montowese, Sicaog (or Suqiang), Tunxis, Podunk, Mahackenos, Massoco, Menunketuck, Poquonnoc, Wongunk, and Mattabesec proper. It will be necessary to discuss these in detail, insofar as possible in geographical order from north to south and from east to west.

### THE MATTABESEC
### The Tunxis Group

On the Farmington River in northern Hartford County there were three subtribes, or sachemdoms, of the Mattabesec. At the mouth were the Poquonnoc, who, according to Hodge (1910: Part II, p. 287), had a village near Windsor. De Forest (1853: p. 46) says that they also had a village five or six miles up the river. Swanton (1952: p. 46) credits them with three villages, Mattianock at the mouth, Poquannoc near the present village of Poquonock, and Mattacomacok. The latter settlement he places near Rainbow on the Farmington River, but refers it erroneously to the Wongunk sachemdom.

Above the Poquonnoc were the Massoco, a subtribe placed by Swanton (1952: p. 46) (but not mentioned by Hodge) as a village near Simsbury. Swanton says that there was also a village called Weataug near Weatogue in Simsbury. Hodge (1910: Part II, p. 927) places this town near Salisbury, Litchfield County, and says that its inhabitants were Mahican. From the facts that Hodge refers only to an item from 1740, and that Weatogue actually is a village near Simsbury, we may conclude that there are two places involved. It follows that there probably was an Indian settlement where Swanton put Weataug.

The third sachemdom is that of the Tunxis, who lived near Farmington at the big bend of the Farmington River. The principal village was near this point, although Swanton (1952: p. 46) names Pequabuck as a Tunxis village near Bristol, and Woodtick as one near Wolcott in New Haven County.

To these three sachemdoms may be added a fourth, which existed in the general area. This tribe was called the Sicaog, in West Hartford, by Hodge (1910: Part II, p. 648). Swanton mentions it only as a village, called Suckiauck, in the Sicaog sachemdom. In the Stiles Documents (Mass. Hist. Soc., Coll., Series 1, Vol. 5, p. 105), we read of Sukiaugk, in West Hartford, "a distinct tribe." In 1730 the people moved to Farmington, and there were two or three families left in 1761. We know of only the one village which belonged to the subtribe.

The number of people who inhabited this region was the cause for comment by local and other contemporary and historical writers. The tunxis seem to have been the most conspicuous band, although they may have been confused with some of the others. In the Stiles Documents (same volume, pp. 112-113) is an article entitled "Indians on Connecticut River." We read: "*Tunxis,* Sepous or Sépous (Farmington) was the largest tribe." In a letter by David McClure (same volume, p. 167) written in 1797 concerning the town of Windsor, we learn that there were three sachem-doms in the vicinity of Windsor, where "the Indians on and near the river were numerous." One of these was at Farmington, about 12 miles west of Windsor. Hodge (1910: Part II, p. 839) points out that the Tunxis sold most of their land in 1640 but that there were 20 wigwams (100 people) left at Farmington in 1700. De Forest (1853: p. 52) in his usual sarcastic vein writes: "If it was worth while to make esti-mates based upon nothing, we might perhaps assign to this tribe a population of eighty to one hundred warriors, or about four hundred individuals." It is worth noting that Mooney (1928: p. 4) accepted De Forest's figure as the aboriginal popu-lation of the Tunxis, although it actually refers to the period not long before King Philip's War.

This timing is important because in the early seventeenth century occurred an epidemic which was one of the most serious which ever afflicted the southern New England Indians. It has been described in detail by Bradford (1897 ed: pp. 387-389) and merits extensive quotation.

In 1632 the Dutch established a trading post at Hartford in order to catch the downriver fur trade. In 1634 some English from Plymouth set up another trading post at or near Windsor. This action is the subject of Bradford's comment:

Ther was a company of people lived in ye country, up above in ye river of Conigtecut, a great way from their trading house ther, and were enimese to those Indeans which lived aboute them, and of whom they stood in some fear (bing a stout people). About a thousand of them had inclosed them selves in a forte, which they had strongly palissadoed about. 3. or 4. Dutch-men went up in ye beginning of winter to live with them, to gett their trade. . . . But their enterprise failed, for it pleased God to visit those Indeans with a great sicknes, and such a mortalitie that of a 1000. above 900. and a halfe of them dyed, and many of them did rott above ground for want of buriall. . . .

This spring (1635) also, those Indeans that lived aboute their trading house there fell sick of ye small poxe, and dyed most miserably; for a sorer disease can not befall them; they fear it more than ye plague. . . .

[Then follows a long description of the course of the disease and the wretched condition of the sufferers. The English at the place did what they could, but] The cheefe Sachem him selfe now dyed & allmost all his friends and kinred.

Certain points emerge from Bradford's account. There were two epidemics. The first was the plague — or it was plague-like in character — and may have been a recurrence of the plague which was so lethal in 1617. The second was smallpox, apparently an extension of the epidemic of 1633. The mortality was very great. Bradford says that 950 out of 1,000 perished. Certainly the proportion cannot be disputed; the absolute number may be. The insistence upon the exposure of 1,000 Indians is supported by the clear statement in a previous line: "About a thousand of them had inclosed them selves in a forte." Whether or not the precise number is correct, Bradford was thinking in terms of 1,000 Indians. A further item to be remembered is that *after* the 950 Indians had died in the first epidemic, the survivors, or perhaps adjacent bands, were subjected to smallpox, and "very few of them escaped."

The tribes involved could have been no other than the four already noted, the Poquonnoc, the Massoco, the Tunxis, and the Sicaog. No others are within the reach of Windsor, except those across the Connecticut River, and there is no indication that they were concerned with events on the west bank.

Two conclusions can be drawn. The first is that a minimum of 1,000 people lived along the Connecticut and Farmington rivers in 1633. This number cannot have included all members of all the sachemdoms. Indeed, the expression "the cheefe Sachem him selfe" implies that only one subtribe was in contact with the English trading post at Windsor. The second conclusion is that the depletion due to these epidemics was tremendous. We do not necessarily have to accept Bradford's 95 percent mortality as exactly applicable, but we cannot reduce the value much below 75 percent, or certainly 50 percent. It follows that any numbers estimated for the subsequent decades, 1635-1675, must be regarded as based upon the residue of the pre-epidemic population.

We return now to the nine villages claimed by Hodge, Swanton, and others. One of these, Tunxis at Farmington, contained most of the members of what had been a large tribe. Pequabuck and Woodtick each may have been one-quarter as large. With De Forest (1853: p. 52) and Mooney (1928: p. 4) agreeing that in the middle of the seventeenth century the Tunxis had 400 people, the main village can have had 250, the smaller settlements 75 each. The tribe suffered very great attrition in the epidemics of 1634-1635, and a factor of two-thirds is not too great. Hence the aboriginal population would have been 1,200.

The Poquonnoc had three villages. We know nothing about their size, except that one was relatively large and the others small. Perhaps a total of 300 persons in the mid-seventeenth century will be adequate, with 900 as the aboriginal number. The Massoco, near Simsbury, probably had two villages. Both would have been relatively small, with, say, 100 inhabitants each. We do not know that this group was stricken by the 1634 epidemics; however, it is difficult to see how they could have escaped. A reasonable depletion factor is one-half. The Massoco would have contained 400 persons in 1630. The fourth subtribe, the Sicaog, apparently had only one village, but the survivors persisted until 1761. The position was exposed, and they may have suffered from the epidemic. If they had 200 persons in 1640, there may have been 400 in 1630.

The estimate for the aboriginal population of the four sachemdoms in the Hartford-Windsor-Farmington area is 2,900. If this number seems excessive, let the reader consider one more quotation from Bradford (p. 402):

Some of their neigbors in ye Bay, hereing of ye fame of Conighticute River, had a hankering mind after it, (as was before noted), and now understanding that ye Indeans were swepte away with ye late great mortalitie, the fear of whom was an obstacle unto them before, which being now taken away, they begane now to presecute it with great egernes.

## The Podunk

Except for the northern few miles, Hartford County, east of the Connecticut River, was occupied by the Podunk sachemdom, concerning whose strength there has been controversy. Hodge (1910: Part II, p. 271) says merely that the Podunk were a small tribe. Ruttenber does not mention them. On the other hand, Swanton (1952: pp. 45-46) lists by name seven villages with their locations, and Spiess (1937) describes six as permanent, together with other temporary villages and camp sites.

The author of the "Indians on Connecticut River" in the Stiles Documents (pp. 112-113) says that the Podunk in King Philip's War contained between two and three hundred men, "who went off in that war and never returned." In addition, he mentions the Hoccanum tribe in East Hartford, which persisted until 1745. Both Swanton (1952: p. 45) and Spiess regard the Hoccanum as part of the Podunk sachemdom, and it is probable that the 200-300 men came from both components. De Forest (1853: pp. 46 and 280) disbelieves the story about these men, calling the estimate "an absurd exaggeration," and saying that it should not be credited. He thinks that the Podunk "could not have mustered more than sixty warriors." Spiess (1937) in his more recent review of the tribe gives evidence to support the opposite view. He says that the tribe was "of moderate size" and quotes the Reverend Woodbridge, who lived many years after 1700 in the area, to the effect that the Podunk had 200 warriors. He puts the total population at 1,500 at this time, a figure which is too high. Two-thirds of that number, say 1,000 for 250 warriors, would be adequate.

We have no clue to the size of the seven villages cited by Swanton (1952: pp. 45-46). However, Spiess gives some idea of their relative importance. The "largest" settlement was at South Windsor. It covered 200 acres, with a fort, and must have held 400 persons, if not more. The "second largest" village was in East Hartford, and can be allowed 250. "Another large" village was in Manchester and covered 15-20 acres, with "still another" village not far away. In the latter there were three rows of 30 fireplaces each. If all the fireplaces were in use simultaneously by single families, a total population of 450 souls would be indicated. We may, however, stay on the conservative side and allow 200 persons each to the Manchester sites. The Hoccanum site was in East Hartford. A large village was situated on the Scantic River near Broad Brook, the home of the Scanticook clan (see Swanton, 1952: p. 46). These two may have contained 100 persons each. The total from the list of Spiess is 1,250. This figure corresponds with the average of 175 which would be required from Swanton's list of seven places, and also with the estimate of warriors who were available in the 1670's.

We still have not allowed for attrition due to disease. There is no evidence that the bands on the east side of the Connecticut River were subjected to violent epidemics in the 1630's, but, on the other hand, it is difficult to see how they could have entirely escaped. Moreover, the information relating to their final disappearance indicates that they suffered from chronic ailments and social disorder, as did all the New England Indians. We may use a factor of one-quarter to allow for erosion prior to 1675, and consider the aboriginal population to have been 1,600.

## The Mattabesec Proper, Wongunk, and Hammonasset

The region south of Hartford to the mouth of the Connecticut River, and including southern Hartford as well as Middlesex County, was occupied by a series of bands or subtribes, concerning whose identity and location there is considerable confusion. Their point of greatest concentration seemed to be at or near Middletown. Hodge (1907: Part I, p. 821) says that here the tribe Mattabesec had their village, of the same name. The Stiles Document, "Indians on Connecticut River" (Mass. Hist. Soc., Coll., Series 1, Vol. 10, p. 105), lists the Mattabesec "or the Middletown tribe at Wongunck on the east side of the Connecticut River." It was "once a great tribe." Swanton (1952: p. 47) says that the village of Pocowset was on the Connecticut River opposite Middletown and was in the Wongunk sachemdom. Hodge (1910: Part II, p. 973) says that Wongunk was a village of the Mattabesec, at Chatham, Connecticut. Chatham is also stated as the seat of the Wongunks by Williamson (1839: Vol. 1, p. 458) and by Sylvester (1910: Vol. 1, p. 52). It is clear that we must move, if possible, from one identifiable village to another.

When we proceed in this manner, we start in the north with Pyquag, which was located at Wethersfield. It was mentioned by several historians, including Hubbard and Trumbull, according to Hodge (1910: Part II, p. 331). Then comes the settlement near Middletown, to which may be added the Montowese. The latter, Hodge says (1907: Part I, p. 939), were on the Connecticut, southwest of Middletown. Montowese appears to have been the name of the chief of these Indians. Hence a band, or a clan is implied. De Forest (1853: p. 55) says that they, the Montowese, had only ten able-bodied men in the tribe. However, it is not clear to what date he is referring. The chief sold the group property in 1638, and the members may have dissipated rapidly and early. In any event they are distinct from the Pocowset, who, according to Swanton (1952: p. 47), inhabited a village on the opposite bank of the Connecticut. There may have been, therefore, a cluster of three, or perhaps more, small villages near Middletown. In the same general vicinity Swanton (1952: pp. 45-46) lists four Wongunk villages, all in Middlesex County not far from Middletown: Cockaponset, Coginchang, Cononnacock, and Machamodus. To the south and southwest, on the lower Connecticut River, lived the Hammonasset, who, according to Hodge (1907: Part I, p. 529), were a small band at Guilford. But Swanton (1952: pp. 45-46) places them more or less along the river in four villages: Pattaquonk at Chester, Pataquasack at Essex, Pocilaug at Westbrook, and Pashesauke at Lyndes Neck.

If we cut through the contradictions we may conclude that in this entire district there were one large village at Wethersfield (Pyquag), one large and three small villages in the vicinity of Middletown (Mattabesec? Pocowset?), and four small villages in the territory of the Hammonasset. This arrangement would argue a concentration of population in the Middletown area, with a thinning out of the inhabitants toward the coast. Such distribution is in conformity with the remarks of Johan de Laet (1625-1640), whose description of the Connecticut Valley in 1614 was republished by Jameson (1909: p. 43). De Laet said: "There are few inhabitants near the mouth of the river, but at the distance of fifteen leagues above they become numerous; their nation is called Sequins." The Sequins were the Mattabesec in the broad sense, and the distances are approximately correct. Above the Sequins were the Nawaas, who in 1614 had a fort at their village. This place was situated in latitude 41°48', almost exactly the latitude of Hartford. They were probably the Podunk.

Regarding attrition of population we have no direct information, although there are numerous indications that the natives along the Connecticut River sold their lands early in the seventeenth century, and sank rapidly into insignificance. Many moved elsewhere and many continued to die until the middle of the eighteenth century, when the survivors were few indeed. The estimates based upon villages — the only estimates we have — must therefore be taken as applying to precolonial conditions. As listed above, there were two large villages, Pyquag at Wethersfield and the one at Middletown, plus seven small villages, three of the Wongunk near Middletown and four of the Hammonasset. If we ascribe 300 souls each to the larger places and 100 each to the smaller, the total is 1,300. This number may be too few, but it is all that can be conservatively estimated.

### The Menunketuck and the Quinnipiack

These two sachemdoms lay to the west of the Hammonasset in what is now central and western New Haven County. The Menunketuck are called a sachemdom by Swanton (1952: p. 46), with a village of the same name at Guilford, Connecticut. Hodge (1907: Part I, p. 844) refers to them as a village at Guilford and says that their land was sold in 1693. Sylvester (1910: Vol. 1, p. 52) lists them as a tribe. Hodge (1910: Part II, p. 344), in the section on the Quinnipiack, suggests that the "Guilford Indians" be included with that tribe. In a similar vein Krzywicki (1934: p. 344) writes: "Perhaps the Indians of Guilford were only a branch of the Quinnipiack, considerably less numerous. . . ." In view of these opinions it will be simplest here to consider the Menunketuck as a subdivision of the Quinnipiack.

The Quinnipiack lived on the Quinnipiac River between New Haven and Meriden. The principal village was located at New Haven. Hodge lists no other, but Swanton (1952: pp. 46-47) lists Mioonktuck, near New Haven, and Totoket, in the nearby town of North Branford.

Various population estimates have been made. De Forest (1853: p. 48) cited records of New Haven Colony from 1638, when the Quinnipiack sold their land. At that time the Indians claimed 47 fighting men, ". . . thus giving . . . a population of two hundred, or possibly two hundred and fifty persons." Krzywicki had the same information (1934: p. 344): "In 1638 the tribe was already reduced to 47 fighting men and about 150 persons in all, Ch. H. Townshend, 11, 24." I have not been able to locate the book by Townshend.[1] Forty years later in 1680 (Krzy-

---

[1] This is probably Charles Hervey Townshend, *A Pictorial History of "Raynham" and Its Vicinity,* New Haven: Tuttle, Morehouse and Taylor Co., 1900-E.V.Y.

wicki from Townshend) there were at least 100 warriors, although some of these may have come from other tribes. The relatively large number indicates that the 1638 figure may be two low.

If we consider villages we have one large tribal center, two small satellites, and one separate village, Menunketuck, which was of sufficient importance to be regarded by some writers as a tribe. Krzywicki (1934: p. 344) says that in 1638 there had already been considerable reduction in numbers, and it is quite probable that this was true. If a factor of four is used, the indicated figures for total population in 1638 and 1680 are respectively 188 and 400. The mean is about 300. The reduction may have been by one-half, and the aboriginal value 600. Alternatively if the principal village had 300, each of the satellites 50, and the Menunketuck 200, the total would be the same – 600 souls.

## The Paugusset

James Mooney, writing in the *Handbook* (1910: Part II, p. 212), says that the Paugusset were a small tribe, although there are data which indicate otherwise. This band occupied the watersheds of the lower Naugatuck and Housatonic rivers in western New Haven and eastern Fairfield Counties. On the coast they extended from west of New Haven to beyond Bridgeport. De Forest (1853: p. 49) says that they covered eight townships in this region. Speck (1928a: pl. 20) on his map indicates that the Naugatuck were a separate tribe, but both Mooney and Swanton list this group as a village subject to the Paugusset.

Swanton (1952: pp. 45-47) names the following villages as in the sachemdom of Paugusset: Capage, near Beacon Falls; Cupheag, at Stratford (but it may be Pisquheege); Meshapack, near Middlebury; Naugatuck, near Naugatuck; Pauquaunuch, in Stratford (the same as Pisquheege); Pisquheege, near Stratford; Pomeraug, near Woodbury; Potatuck, one or two towns in Newton; Squantuck, on the Housatonic River above Derby; Turkey Hill, near Derby, perhaps listed under another name; Wepawaug, near Milford; Woronoke, another name for Wepawaug. If we eliminate the duplications there are at least eight villages, separate from each other, but of recognized existence. Mooney, in the *Handbook* (1910: Part II, p. 212), says that apart from their principal village they had Turkey Hill, Pauquaunuch, Naugatuck, and Poodatook. These are probably included in Swanton's list. The Paugusset also had two forts, one on the Housatonic River just above the Naugatuck, and another in Milford.

There are several estimates of population. Mooney, in the *Handbook* (1910: Part II, p. 212), says that the principal village had about 300 inhabitants, and with four other villages the whole tribe numbered perhaps 700 or 800. With a total of 750, the four smaller villages would have averaged 110 each.

A very interesting pseudo-count was made by the Reverend Nathan Birdsey, who wrote to Rev. E. Stiles from Stratford under date of September 3, 1761. The letter dealt with the Indian population of 50 years earlier, i.e., 1710, and was confined principally to the lower Housatonic River (Mass. Hist. Soc., Coll., Series 1, Vol. 10, pp. 111-112). Birdsey says that at Paugusset "by Derby ferry and against Derby neck" 50 years previously there were 8 or 10 wigwams, "containing 10 or

12 families." This means about 60 people. At Turkey Hill, also near Derby, there were 8 or 10 families, or about 50 persons. In the next paragraph Birdsey says: "There were at Pauquaunuch, i.e., Stratfield [this must be an error for Stratford], the place called Golden Hill, about 20 or 25 wigwams 50 years ago. And in several other parts of the town there were small clans of two or three wigwams." The total wigwams at Stratford were close to 30, or nearly 200 people. Hence in Derby and Stratford there was a total residual Indian population of 310 souls.

In his final sentence Birdsey says: "I suppose in the whole bounds of Stratford 50 years ago, the best calculation that can be made of their numbers is about 60 or 70, perhaps 80 fighting men." The estimated population would again come close to 300. Meanwhile Birdsey remarks: "At Poodatook by the river against Newton [ten to fifteen miles above Derby on the Housatonic], I have been lately informed by some Newtown people, when Newtown was first settled, a little above 50 years ago, there were reckoned of that tribe 50 fighting men." The population there would have been about 200.

It follows from these statements that in 1710 the remnant of the Paugusset in the Housatonic Valley amounted to a minimum of 500 souls. If the Birdsey letter of 1710 is correct — and it bears the mark of a sensible survey — the Paugusset had been reduced from 750 to 500 since the period 1670-1680; the probable time of the Mooney estimate. This leaves room for severe depletion during the interval 1610-1670. A rule of thumb, but a reasonable estimate, would yield a factor of one-half, and an aboriginal population of 1,500.

Swanton's (1952: pp. 45-46) list of eight villages is of assistance here. The Paugusset had two forts, or palisaded villages. These were of such importance that the inhabitants could not have numbered less than 300 each. The other six villages were smaller but must have reached the range of 100-200 persons, say an average of 150. The total aboriginal population would have amounted to 1,500, or the same as we estimated from the Birdsey count of 1710 and the Mooney estimate from an earlier date.

### THE UNCOWA, THE TANKITEKE, THE SIWANOY

It is clear that with these, as with all the Wappinger subtribes in this area, the exact boundaries are unknown. A great deal of confusion exists among the students who have written about these Indians, such that statements concerning occupation of specific modern townships and counties are conflicting and contradictory. The primary cause of the difficulty is the fact that the natives themselves had no fixed boundaries and that there was much interdigitation of lands used for agriculture and hunting. A secondary cause is the pressure put on the natives at an early date by the Dutch and the English, with the consequence that the settlement sites were repeatedly shifted.

This condition prejudices any attempt to assess population levels, particularly because for the Siwanoy and many other divisions of the Wappinger Confederacy there are no reports which show actual numbers for the natives, even at a date long past the first arrival of the whites. With the exception of the Weckquaesgeek, there were no serious battles which evoked estimates of number, there were no counts, and there was no attempt to organize congregations. The result is that we are forced to fall back upon the number and the probable size of recorded villages and other settlements. However, here again we encounter discrepancy among the historians, which is induced basically by the inability to define boundaries with acceptable accuracy.

The difficulties of the historians are important because, with the exception of the Manhattan, the Dutch and English documents relating to the period 1610-1670 are of little assistance, and there is no source to which we can turn which dates back farther than 1870, when Ruttenber wrote his book. Robert Bolton (1881) compiled a vast array of detail concerning Westchester County, although the reliability of his data is variable. Hodge's *Handbook* of 1907 and 1910 summarizes much of what was known at that time, and Swanton in 1952 put together an extensive subtribe and village list, which presumably represents the core of what we shall ever know concerning these entities. In seeking to evaluate population, it becomes necessary to work with these recent sources and to reconcile as many of their different presentations as possible.

The Uncowa (or Unkawa) were a subtribe according to Speck (1928a: pl. 20), or a village according to Swanton (1952: p. 47). The latter says that they were in the Tankiteke sachemdom. Hodge (1910: Part II, p. 819) calls them a "small band" and says that they lived near Fairfield, Connecticut.

The Tankiteke are mentioned by Hodge (1910: Part II, p. 686) as a Wappinger tribe in Westchester County, New York, and back of the coast in Fairfield County, Connecticut. They are chieftaincy no. 5 of Ruttenber (1872: p. 80) and occupied Darien, Stamford, and New Canaan in Connecticut, together with Poundridge, Bedford, and Greenbush in Westchester County, New York. Bolton (1881: Vol. 1, p. vii) says that they "resided in the rear of Sing Sing" — which is one way of putting it. They disappeared early, for they sold their land in 1641. Nevertheless they are shown as the Pachami on Van Der Donck's map of 1656 (see Jameson, 1909: p. 294) and are stated by de Laet in 1615 (Jameson, 1909: p. 46) to have been dwelling on the east bank of the Hudson River.

The best village list for both groups is that of Swanton (1952: pp. 45-47), who mentions Aspetuck, near the town of the same name, 5 or 10 miles northwest of Bridgeport; Pahquiske, near Danbury; Ramopo, near Ridgefield; Saugatuck, near the mouth of the Saugatuck River; Titicus, in the town of Ridgefield; Unkowa, mentioned here above; Weantinock, near Fairfield; and Werawang, near Danbury. It is noteworthy that all these villages are in Fairfield County, Connecticut, whereas both Hodge and Ruttenber indicate that the tribe extended well into Westchester County. Either Swanton missed some New York villages or the tribe had gravitated eastward by the time Swanton's villages flourished. However, it is probable that the tribe did possess as many as eight villages in 1620, irrespective of their exact location.

The Siwanoy were chieftaincy no. 7 of the Wappingers, according to Ruttenber's (1872: p. 77) classification. They lived on the north shore of Long Island Sound

between Norwalk, Connecticut, and the Bronx. Although they are said to have
extended inland as far as White Plains, New York, they were bordered on the interior by the Tankiteke, who may have been simply a subdivision of the Siwanoy.

Ruttenber (1872: p. 81) calls the Siwanoy one of the largest of the Wappinger
divisions. He has found deeds from them conveying land in a long series of towns:
Pelham, New Rochelle, East and West Chester, North and New Castle, Mamaroneck,
Scarsdale, White Plains, West Farms, Rye, and Harrison, New York, and Stamford,
Connecticut. Bolton (1881: Vol. 1, p. 403) confirms the occupation in Mamaroneck,
New Rochelle, Pelham, and Rye.

With respect to the size of these settlements, it is generally stated that the
Siwanoy had a village at or near Rye, which Ruttenber (1872: p. 81) says was "very
large." Bolton (1881: Vol. 2, p. 127), Hodge (1910: Part II, p. 279), and Swanton
(1952: p. 45) all confirm its existence, and Hodge calls it the principal village.
There was also a castle, or fort, in the same vicinity. Whether it was part of the same
settlement is not clear. In any event, its presence may be associated with Ruttenber's
description as "very large." We have usually considered large villages to have contained approximately 300 persons. A very large village, in conjunction with a castle,
must have held up to 500 souls, particularly if it was the principal village of a sizable subtribe.

According to Ruttenber (1872: p. 87), a second village was located at Daven-
port's Neck. It was called Shippa by Bolton (1881: Vol. 1, p. 581) and placed at
New Rochelle; it was called Shippan by Swanton (1952: p. 47) and placed in
Stamford. Nothing is said about its size, but it must have been reasonably large,
let us say with 300 inhabitants. Two other castles are mentioned: the castle "of
the Siwanoy" in the village of East Chester (Bolton, 1881: Vol. 1, p. 202) and
the one at Castle Hill Neck in West Chester (Ruttenber, 1872: p. 81). It is not
clear whether these were associated with villages, although castles or forts generally
were. In view of the lack of concrete evidence, we shall not ascribe any population
to them.

Other designated villages include one "about Bear Swamp," mentioned by Ruttenber (1872: p. 81), and three in Norwalk and Greenwich, Connecticut, listed by
Swanton (1952: pp. 46-47). We may assume their existence but consider them to
have been relatively small. An average of 100 souls would be adequate. The total
estimate for the Siwanoy would therefore reach 1,200 persons.

For the Tankiteke, as was noted above, Swanton lists eight villages, including
the Uncowa. The Uncowa can certainly be credited with 100 persons in 1620. However, if the same number were inhabitants of the other seven villages, the total
would amount to 800 souls. This seems a large number for what may have been
only a splinter group of the Siwanoy. To reduce the value is somewhat arbitrary,
but it seems called for under the circumstances. The population assigned to the
Tankiteke, therefore, is 600, and that for the entire Siwanoy-Tankiteke group is
1,800.

## THE SINT-SINK, THE KITCHAWANC, THE NOCHPEEM, AND THE WAPPINGER PROPER

These are four of Ruttenber's (1872: p. 77) chieftaincies, nos. 3, 4, 6, and 9, respectively. They all occupied land in New York State, in Westchester, Putnam, and southern Dutchess Counties. They are characterized, with one exception, by the absence of any direct numerical data concerning population, although their names appear with comment in the work of both Hodge (1907, 1910) and Swanton (1952: pp. 45-47). We must therefore rely upon records of the villages inhabited.

The Sint-sink are included as a sachemdom by Swanton (1952: p. 45), but he mentions no villages under this subtribe, unless we include Ossingsing, located at Ossining, New York. Both Ruttenber (1872: p. 79) and Hodge (1910: Part II, pp. 161, 676) however, are very explicit in referring the village Kestaubuinck to the Sint-sink, along with Ossingsing. Since both villages were of some consequence, although Ruttenber (1872: p. 79) says "this chieftaincy does not appear to have been very numerous," a combined population of 400 should be adequate.

The Kitchawanc are stated by Hodge (1907, I: p. 705) to have been a small tribe in Westchester County, although Ruttenber (1872: p. 79) says that they extended up the Hudson River from the Croton River to Anthony's Nose. Ruttenber (1872: p. 79) also says that their principal village was Kitchawonk, at the mouth of the Croton River, and Bolton (1881: Vol. 1, pp. 83-84) calls it one of the principal villages of Westchester County. Ruttenber (1872: p. 79), Bolton (1881: Vol. 1, p. 84), and Hodge (1910: Part II, p. 462) all mention a second village, Sackhoe, at Peekskill. Swanton (1952: p. 46) also lists Senesqua at the mouth of the Croton River, but Ruttenber (1872: p. 79) and Hodge (1910: Part II, p. 502) describe the place as the location of the fort or castle, without mention of a village. It appears consequently that there were only two villages, one evidently large, the other probably smaller. With 300 persons in one and 200 in the other, the total would be 500.

The Nochpeem were chieftaincy no. 6 of Ruttenber (1872: p. 77). He says that they lived in the highlands north of Anthony's Nose. Hodge (1910: Part II, p. 79) places them near Matteawan (now part of Beacon) in Dutchess County. Swanton (1952: p. 46) says merely that they were in the southern part of Dutchess County. Their villages were shown on Van Der Donck's map (see Jameson, 1909: pp. 294-295) as Nochpeem, Keskistkonck, and Pasquasheck, names which are repeated by Ruttenber, Hodge (1907: Part I, p. 676; 1910: Part II, p. 207), and Swanton. Nochpeem is stated by Bolton (1881: p. vii) to have been one of the principal villages of Westchester County. On the other hand Ruttenber (1872: p. 50) says, and Hodge repeats the idea: "Their principal village, however, appears to have been called Canopus, from the name of their sachem." It is doubtful whether the tribe had two principal villages; but rather there were probably one principal and three secondary settlements. If so, and if we allow 300 for the former, and 300 for the latter collectively, the total becomes 600.

Just how the Wappinger proper were constituted is obscure. Hodge (1910: Part II, p. 913) lists them as the leading tribe of the Wappinger Confederacy, who occu-

pied the territory around Poughkeepsie. Bolton (1881: Vol. 1, p. 164) says that
they occupied the highlands in the vicinity of Anthony's Nose; "their principal settlement, designated Wickopy, was situated in the vicinity of Anthony's Nose." Swanton (1952: p. 45) says that the Wappinger proper were "about Poughkeepsie in
Dutchess County, New York." However, he lists no villages for them. Ruttenber
has the best account. According to him (1872: pp. 83-84) they were north of the
highlands and were "acknowledged as the head of the chieftaincies of the tribal organization of that name." He then points out that "on Van der Donck's map three of
their villages or castles are located on the south side of Mawenawasigh, or Great Wappinger's Kill, which now bears their name." But Van Der Donck's map (see
Jameson, 1909: pp. 294-295) shows only three faint dots, with no names or ex-
planation. It is very likely, however, that three settlements of some kind were there.

Ruttenber then mentions the names of two chiefs, one of whom he discusses
further in a footnote (1872: p. 84, n. 1). There is a quotation from New York Land
Papers, XVIII, 127 (no date given) to the effect that Daniel Numham, "a native
Indian and acknowledged sachem or king of a certain tribe of Indians known and
called by the name of *Wappingers* represents that the tribe formerly were numerous,
at present consists of about two hundred and twenty seven persons." The Christian
name and the general tenor of the document indicate that it was written toward the
end of the seventeenth century, or possibly as late as 1700. The tract of land con-
veyed lay in the present towns near Fishkill in Dutchess County.

It is apparent that we have a record of sorts for four villages. If they were of the
usual size, 600-800 persons might have inhabited them. The formula used in the land
grant, however, implies that after severe depletion the tribe still contained 227 persons. If the reduction had been by two-thirds, not an improbable amount, the
original level would have been at 682, or let us say 700. The village data and the
depletion estimate thus coincide.

THE WECKQUAESGEEK

This sachemdom contained two villages and three castles. The village of Weckquaesgeek was located at Dobbs Ferry, and Alipconck was at Tarrytown. However,
the holdings of this subtribe included Mt. Pleasant, Greenburg, White Plains, and
Rye, New York, and extended across to Norwalk, Connecticut, according to Ruttenber (1872: p. 78). The two villages might have accommodated 600-700 persons.

Apart from the number and size of villages, we have information bearing on the
Weckquaesgeek from reports of the Dutch War of 1643-1644. In another place
(Cook, 1973b: p. 10) I have discussed the extent of casualties following the attack
by the Dutch and English on one of the villages, where a large number of Indians
had gathered for a festival. The massacre was barbarous, but the point of interest
here is that nearly 1,000 Indians were said to have been present. If this total included the entire tribe, as well it may have, then the number of members in 1644
may be set at 1,000. If representatives from other tribes were present as visitors,
we have no word of it.

Another matter is of concern. This attack was made on a village in Greenwich, Connecticut, or at least no more than a short day's march from that town. No modern writer mentions such a village, yet that it existed is clear from the circumstantial account, quoted by Ruttenber (1872: pp. 115-116) of its arrangement and houses. The question is immediately raised: How many other villages were there in Wappinger territory which have escaped the notice of modern chroniclers? Also, what of the normal population of this village? The Ruttenber account says that there were three rows of houses, each 80 paces long. This is 240 yards, or 720 feet. With one "house" every 20 feet there were 36 houses. With eight occupants each there were 288 people. This figure is very close to the 300 which we have been allowing for a "large" village.

Villages cannot be conjured up where there is no record of them. But with the Weckquaesgeek we can assume three, not two, with a total population of 900 souls.

### THE MANHATTAN

This otherwise insignificant subtribe has reached the apogee of notoriety by virtue of its sale to the Dutch of Manhattan Island and the site of the future center of New York City. These Indians occupied not only Manhattan Island but the east bank of the Hudson River as far north as Yonkers. They constituted the first chieftaincy of the Wappingers (although Swanton [1952: p. 49] lists them under the Delaware) and are called by Ruttenber (1872: p. 77) the Reckgawawancs. The term Manhattan is applied to those Indians encountered on the island, who were but part of the entire tribe. The principal village was known as Nappachamak and was located at Yonkers. Their fort or castle was Nipinichsen, on the north bank of Spuyten Duyvil Creek, and was quite distinct from the village. In addition, a number of temporary fishing and camp sites were maintained on Manhattan Island. These temporary gathering places undoubtedly had been established for many years and in large measure account for the numerous shell middens and other archaeological sites which have been described in the vicinity of New York City. The subtribe, therefore, according to all reports, possessed only one permanent village, to which may be ascribed a tentative population of 300 souls.

Since this region was opened up relatively early by the Dutch, there are a few direct indications of the number of Indians. Robert Juet (see Jameson, 1909: p. 19), writing in 1610, described how Henry Hudson entered the river of his name. On September 6, off Manhattan Island, two canoes came out from shore, with twelve men in one and fourteen in the other. Later, on September 12, there came out 28 canoes filled with men, women, and children (Jameson, 1909: p. 20). If there were fourteen persons in each canoe, the total was 392, probably the entire tribe.

Isaak de Rasières (see Jameson, 1909: p. 103), in his letter to Samuel Blommaert, written in 1628, described Manhatten Island. "It is inhabited by the old Manhatans (Manhatesen); they are almost 200 to 300 strong, women and men." Subsequently he remarked concerning Manhattan Island: "In some places there is a little good land, where formerly many people have dwelt, but who for the most part have died or have been driven away by the Wappanos" (p. 105). It is clear, consequently, that the 200-300 found in 1628 had already suffered significant reduction, and that the 392, or 400, seen in 1609 represented the aboriginal population. This finding is in effect confirmed by the newer data which refer to known villages.

CONCLUSION

For the component parts of the Wappinger Confederacy, including almost all the land in Connecticut and New York between the Connecticut and Hudson Rivers, we get the following estimate:

| | | | |
|---|---|---|---|
| Tunxis group | 2,900 | Kitchawanc | 500 |
| Podunk | 1,600 | Nochpeem | 600 |
| Mattabesec-Wongunk group | 1,300 | Wappinger proper | 700 |
| Menunketuck and Quinnipiack | 600 | Weckquaesgeek | 900 |
| Paugusset | 1,500 | Manhattan | 400 |
| Siwanoy group | 1,800 | | |
| Sint-sink | 400 | *Total* | 13,200 |

A final estimate relates to the density of the population. The area is roughly that between the Connecticut and the Hudson rivers south of the 42nd parallel. However, there must be added the land east of the Connecticut which belonged to the Podunk, Mattabesec proper, and Wongunk opposite Hartford and Middletown. Furthermore, the northern boundary runs in a more or less sinuous line from Windsor Locks west and southwest so as to include the Farmington Valley and the region just north of Waterbury. From this point it runs slightly north of west to Poughkeepsie on the Hudson River. Obviously there can be no precise delineation of boundaries in the interior.

By planimeter measurement this territory comprises approximately 3,120 square miles, or, if preferred, the range 3,000-3,200 square miles. The density, using the more exact figure given, is 4.2 persons per square mile, or we may be satisfied with the range 4.0-4.5 persons per square mile. This value is of the same order of magnitude as has been found for the mainland tribes further east, and indicates a broad uniformity of environment in southern New England east of the Hudson River.

Chapter 6

# THE UPPER HUDSON VALLEY AND LONG ISLAND

## THE MAHICAN

In the early seventeenth century, at the time of Dutch and English occupation of New England and the Hudson Valley, the Mahican, or as the French called them, the Loups, occupied the east bank of the Hudson River north of Poughkeepsie almost to Lake Champlain and eastward into Massachusetts and Connecticut. They had but recently come from the west and were existing in what was apparently a state of unstable equilibrium with the Iroquois to the north and west. They were subjected to continuous pressure from these tribes and also from the Europeans until, in the decades 1660 to 1680, they moved eastward into the upper Housatonic Valley. Here they established new settlements and came under the Christianizing influence of Puritan and Moravian missionaries. This uninterrupted movement from a time before the arrival of the white man would make very difficult, under the best of statistical circumstances, any evaluation of their precontact population. As Mooney and Thomas say (*Handbook,* 1907: Part I, p. 787): "It is impossible to estimate their population, as the different bands were always confounded or included with neighboring tribes, of whom they afterward became an integral part."

A second reason for difficulty in estimating aboriginal population is our almost complete ignorance of the political history of the Mahican. The contemporary Dutch documents tell little about the subtribes and villages, and the French documents even less. A thorough scanning of the long series "Documents Relative to the Colonial History of the State of New York," published between 1853 and 1887, has yielded no information of pertinence. The first modern work of importance is that of Ruttenber (1872), who made a careful survey of all data available at that time. His conclusions, especially with regard to the subdivisions which he himself established, are interesting (1872: pp. 86-87):

> But these subdivisions are of no practical importance. In tribal action they were as unknown as the merest hamlet in the voice of a civilized state. . . . Had the lands upon which they were located been sold in small tracts and opened to settlement at an early period, they would not have escaped observation and record; but the wilderness was a sealed book for many years, and there are those who still write that it was without Indian habitations.

We may concede that Ruttenber assembled all the data available at his time. Subsequently a substantial article was written by James Mooney and Cyrus Thomas in the *Handbook,* 1907: Part I, pp. 786-788. These authors, however, added little to Ruttenber's account. A more recent review is that of Swanton (1952), whose Mahican lists (pp. 41-42) are taken from those of his predecessors. Consideration has been given at length to the problems of the Mahican by Allen W. Trelease (1960) in his book on Indian affairs in New York during the seventeenth century. The key works on the Mahican, nevertheless, remain that of Ruttenber and that of Mooney and Thomas.

Village lists for the Mahican are badly defective. Ruttenber (1872: pp. 85-89) names five subtribes, or divisions, one of which was on the west side of the Hudson River, but he makes no attempt to mention villages for the early phases of their history. Mooney and Thomas (Hodge, 1907: Part I, p. 788) list eleven villages as having been recorded, and Swanton lists fourteen. However, many of these, perhaps more than half, are dated from the eighteenth century, or at least after the Mahican had moved in part to the Housatonic Valley. Consequently they are useless for the establishment of the aboriginal population.

Ruttenber (1872: p. 80), after mentioning a few known Mahican settlements, comments on their probable real number: "That their villages and chieftaincies were even more numerous than those of the *Montauks* and *Wappingers* there is every reason to suppose. . . ." He reinforces this idea with a footnote (1872: p. 86, n. 6): "Local research would, it is believed, develope forty villages in the territory of the Mahicans." Mooney and Thomas endorse this estimate when they say (1907: Part I, p. 786): ". . . and it is probable that they had 40 villages within their territory."

Some notion of the size of the villages may be obtained from the account given by Mooney and Thomas. These authors (Hodge, 1907: Part I, p. 787) state that: "Their houses were of the communal sort and differed usually only in length." The width was about twenty feet and the maximum length 180 feet. The average length probably was about eighty feet. This size would accommodate at least four families of five persons each, or twenty persons per house. It must be borne in mind, of course, that these dimensions pertain only to the Mahican, not to New England tribes, although the description resembles those given for the neighboring Iroquois.

Mooney and Thomas go on to describe the castles, or forts, which "not infrequently" contained twenty or thirty houses. It follows that a fortified village of twenty houses with twenty occupants each would hold 400 people, a size which we have, in previous discussion, considered a large settlement. From this figure an approximate calculation is possible.

According to Ruttenber (1872: pp. 86-87), one of the five divisions of the Mahican was located on the west side of the Hudson River and therefore should be omitted from consideration. On the east side Ruttenber mentions four castles and six villages which were known to the Dutch. If we make moderate allowance for unrecorded castles, we may consider that they had six. If Ruttenber's guess is within the range of the truth, and if one-fifth of the tribe lived to the west of the Hudson, then there would have been 32 villages on the east side. Of these, six would have been attached to the castles. Six castles at 400 persons each sum to 2,400 souls, and 26 villages at no more than 100 each sum to 2,600. The total is 5,000. If the villages are thought of as larger, the population estimate is greater.

Some indication of the number of Mahican who survived the prolonged and bitter warfare with the Iroquois during the seventeenth century may be gleaned from a few references found in the official correspondence of 1680-1690, as reported in the series entitled "Documents Relative to the Colonial History of the State of New York," Vol. 9, 1855.

In 1684 Rev. Jean de Lamberville wrote to M. de la Barre (p. 259): "Six or seven hundred Mohegans [Loups] were preparing to go to the assistance of the Iroquois. . . ."

In the same year the same writer said (p. 261) that an Indian said that there were 1,200 Loups between "Marinland" and New York.

In the *Narrative of the Most Remarkable Occurrences in Canada, 1689, 1690* (p. 473), written by M. de Monseignat, there is described an expedition by the French: "They did not think it prudent to go any farther, having learned that there were seven hundred Mohegans [Loups] a day and a half's journey off who were in wait for them. . ."

On p. 476 of the same document a fight is described in which 40 Abnaki routed 600 men [presumably Mohicans, or Loups].

On pp. 1052-1058 of the same volume is a document entitled *Enumeration of the Indian Tribes Connected with the Government of Canada,* from about 1725, attributed to de Chauvignerie, in which occurs the statement: "The Mohegans [Loups] who understand the Abenakis, and whom the Abenakis understand, are dispersed from Boston to Virginia. . . . This nation may be six hundred men, under British rule."

It is clear that in 1680-1690, unless these officials were lying — and there is no reason why they should have been — the Mahican disposed of 600-1,200 warriors, the exact number obviously indeterminate. At the usual ratio of 1:4 this number implies a total population of 2,400-4,800.

Another passage is worth quoting. This is in the same volume (p. 490) and is again from the *Narrative* of M. de Monseignat for 1689-1690. He says that some Abnaki, arriving from Acadia, reported on the great smallpox epidemic which had killed 400 Iroquois and 100 "Mohegans": ". . . and that in the great Mohegan town where they had been, only sixteen men had been spared by the disease." Apart from the terrible effect of this epidemic the expression "great Mohegan town" is noteworthy.

These are all hearsay statements. Nevertheless, they do support the thesis that the Mahican, even after suffering from protracted warfare and blighting epidemics, maintained a substantial population. Consequently, if there were 2,500 left in 1690 there must have been at least 5,000 in 1610.

It might be possible to get an estimate from density values. However, in addition to the difficulty in getting a firm figure for population, the occupied area cannot be determined with precision. Especially on the north and northeast the boundary is extremely hazy. Moreover, the limits of the group on the west bank of the Hudson River cannot be drawn with even an approach to accuracy. It is true that we can guess. Thus, if the density is the same as that of the Wappinger, approximately 4.0 persons per square mile, and the territory occupied covers 1,000 square miles, the population is 4,000. If the territory covers 1,500 square miles, the population is 6,000. It is useless to attempt such estimates beyond establishing the probability that the population was in the low thousands. The minimum appears to lie at Mooney's (1928: p. 4) estimate of 3,000. The maximum may reach 6,000 or 7,000. We shall use 5,000 as a purely tentative estimate, and undertake to make a more thorough examination of the tribe in the future.

## THE LONG ISLAND INDIANS

The natives of Long Island were associated with both New England and New York. In some respects, particularly with regard to the sources of knowledge concerning them, they are a part of the complex of tribes which inhabited southern New York. On the other hand, they lived east of the Hudson River and were only a few miles off the Connecticut coast. Hence they may on geographical grounds be included with the Indians of New England.

The size of the aboriginal population is completely unknown. In fact, the usual traditions and guesses are absent. They never engaged in full-scale war with the whites or for the whites, and consequently even the number of their warriors has never been estimated. Yet it has been recognized since the seventeenth century that Long Island was heavily occupied by Indians. Perhaps one difficulty is that we are dealing with the population which inhabited a geographic area, rather than with a specific political or tribal unit whose fortunes may be followed at least to some extent from the time of first contact with the white man.

Aside from references to strictly local events, the status of very restricted groups, and a few scattered land purchases with accompanying legal documents, there is no comprehensive study available which treats of the Indians as a separate racial entity. Perhaps we ought to except the brief summaries of tribal divisions which were presented by Wood (1828), Thompson (1839), Prime (1845), and Ruttenber (1872), for these must form the basis of any consideration of tribes, villages, and settlements. Even Mooney, in the *Handbook* (1907: Part I, pp. 934-935) devotes less than a page of text to the principal tribe, the Montauk, although he allows a total population of 6,000 Indians for the island in his article of 1928 (p. 4). The Long Island Indians as a whole he discusses in the short section (*Handbook,* 1907: Part I, p. 851) on the Metoac. Mooney's estimate has drawn comment from Trelease (1960: p. 5), who thinks that 6,000 shows a "comparatively heavy population." To this point of view may be added the statement of Wood (1828: pp. 61-62), made over a century earlier, that "the whole Indian population was considerable, but by no means as great as the facilities for subsistence would have authorized us to expect, nor as great as it probably had formerly been."

The number of villages is unknown. Hodge (1907: Part I, p. 851) lists 20 named villages. Swanton (1952: pp. 42-43) lists twelve "subdivisions" of the Montauk, and names or locates twenty villages, some of which carry the same name as the subdivisions. I have seen no estimate which exceeds this figure, and yet twenty villages must have represented an underestimate.

The subtribes, divisions, or bands which lived on Long Island appear to have been the following. Here I follow the list of Ruttenber (1872: p. 72) who calls the divisions "chieftaincies" of the Montauk.

## Canarsee

"They were formerly one of the leading tribes on Long Island. . ." (Hodge, 1907: Part I, p. 199), and occupied most of Kings County (Brooklyn) and part of Jamaica. Swanton does not mention them because he considers that they did not belong to the Montauk Confederacy. Their principal village was at Flatlands. Hodge also mentions two other villages, at Maspeth and at Hempstead. Thompson (1839: pp. 66ff.) says that their numbers must have been considerable. The villages would amount to three, one principal and two subsidiary.

## Rockaway

This was a tribe living around Rockaway and the southern part of Hempstead. Their principal village was Rechquaakie, near Rockaway. Thompson (1839: pp. 66ff.) says that they had other settlements at the head of Maspeth Creek in Newtown, and on Hog Island in Rockaway Bay, and he is likely to be correct. Hence there were three villages, one principal and two subsidiary.

## Merric

Hodge (1907: Part I, p. 845) says that this was a small tribe on the south shore of the island from Rockaway to South Oyster Bay. According to Ruttenber (1872: p. 73), and there is no statement to the contrary, they had one village at Merick or Mericks (the present-day Merrick). Thompson (1839: p. 139) thinks that they were formerly part of the Massapequa division. Swanton (1952: p. 43) mentions Merric both as a division and as a village.

## Massapequa

This group also held land on the south shore of Long Island around Seaford and Babylon, from Fort Neck east to Islip. Their chief village was at Fort Neck, where Ruttenber (1872: p. 73) says that they had two forts. This concentration of force bespeaks two supporting villages, or else one very large one. Hodge (1907: Part I, p. 817) quotes Flint, *Early Long Island* (1896), as saying that the Indians had built a fort "capable of holding 500 men." Such a number would imply a total of 2,000 souls. Although this may be an exaggeration, it will not be unreasonable to count the aggregate as two villgaes of more than average size. Swanton (1952: p. 43) lists Massapequa as both a division and a village.

## Matinecoc

They were a tribe on northwestern Long Island, occupying the area from Newton, Queens County, to Smithtown, Suffolk County. All authorities agree that they were, or had been, numerous, although the governor of New York, Van Tienhoven, in 1650 (Docs. Rel. Col. Hist. New York, Vol. 1, p. 366) said that there were but thirty families, or approximately 200 people, left. The governor also described the village "where they have their plantation . . . in and about this bay, great numbers of Indian plantations, which now lie waste and vacant." Thompson (1839: pp. 66ff.) says that they had several large settlements at Flushing, Glen Cove, Cold Spring Harbor, Huntington, and Cow Harbor. Ruttenber (1872: p. 73) also mentions these places as "large villages." We have, then, Van Tienhoven's general statements and Thompson's specific itemization of five villages. This number must be tentatively accepted.

## Nesaquake

This tribe held the country in the northern half of the island from Nesaquake River to Stony Brook. The Matinecoc retired here after the war of 1643 (see p. 000 below), but there seems always to have been a settlement near the present village of Nesaquake. This tribe is omitted by Wood (1828) but is included by

Thompson (1839: pp. 66ff.) and by Swanton (1952: p. 43) as a subdivision and a village, and by others as well. Apparently there never was more than a single village.

## Setauket

These people lived on the north shore of Long Island from Stony Brook to Wading River. Their main village was on Little Neck. They disappeared early, for they sold their last land in 1675. Thompson (1839: pp. 66ff.) describes them as "one of the most powerful tribes in the county," and Ruttenber (1872: p. 74) remarks that they were "said to have been a numerous family" Nevertheless, only one village can be ascribed to them.

## Corchaug

Thompson (1839: pp. 66ff.) and Ruttenber (1872: p. 74) place this division as lying between Wading River and Oyster Ponds, including the north shore of Peconic Bay. Hodge (1907: Part I, p. 348) puts them in Riverhead and Southold townships of Suffolk County. Ruttenber (1872: p. 74) describes them "as regards numbers and military power, a respectable clan," but he mentions none of their villages. On the other hand, both Hodge and Swanton (1952: p. 43) name four villages: Cutchogue, Mattituck, Ashamomuck, and Aquebogue. These may be considered as of over average size.

## Manhasset

Hodge (1907: Part I, p. 800) describes them as "a small band of the Montauk group living at Shelter Island" at the east end of Long Island. There is apparently a difference of opinion because Thompson wrote (1839: p. 66): "This tribe, although confined to about 10,000 acres could, as tradition affirms, bring into the field more than 500 fighting men." This statement is repeated by Ruttenber (1872: p. 74). Five hundred warriors would mean a total population of 2,000 souls. On 10,000 acres the density would be almost 130 persons per square mile, a wholly improbable contingency. One sizable village is all that can be credited to them.

## Secatogue

Here was a tribe, or division, which lived on the south shore of Long Island between South Oyster Bay and Patchogue, with the principal village at or near Islip. The tribe was badly depleted when the whites arrived. As Ruttenber (1872: p. 75) says: "They were so much reduced by wars and disease that when settlements were made among them their lands were comparatively deserted." Only one village has ever been mentioned as possessed by them.

## Patchogue

The Patchogue were a tribe on the south shore of Long Island from Patchogue to Westhampton. Thompson (1839: pp. 66ff.) says that their principal settlements "must have been" Patchogue, Fireplace, Mastic, Mariches, and Westhampton. This list is repeated verbatim by Ruttenber (1872: p. 75), Hodge (1910: Part II,

p. 209), and Swanton (1952: pp. 42-43). If we may rely upon Thompson there were indeed five villages, but it is doubtful if they were all of the maximum size. Purely as an estimate we may call two of them large and three small.

## Shinnecock

This tribe, or band, occupied the south shore from Shinnecock Bay to Montauk Point, including the south shore of Peconic Bay. There were a few members left in 1905 who lived on a reservation just west of Southampton. Swanton (1952: p. 43) lists the division but gives no villages. Indeed, no settlements are known by name, although at least one village must have existed.

## Montauk

In the broad sense this name applied to all the tribes of Long Island except the westernmost, the Canarsee. In the restricted sense the name refers to the tribe which occupied Easthampton, Montauk Point, and Gardiner's Island. The chief, or sachem, of the tribe, at one time at least, controlled the other divisions. The Montauk appear to have been, as Ruttenber says, considerable in numbers. Even after the smallpox epidemic of 1658-1659 the survivors were estimated at 500 persons. Their principal village, and the only one mentioned specifically as far as I can determine, was at Fort Pond, near Montauk Point. If it was the only settlement — and one would suppose that there were more — it must have been a large one. However, no others are known by name.

I have sketched above thirteen subtribes, or divisions of the Long Island Indians, who lived in 29 known settlements. Of these, 22 may be regarded as substantial or large; the remainder are of doubtful or small size. Some of the thirteen divisions have been described as populous, others as relatively small. A few held as many as several hundred persons even after severe depletion; others had almost disappeared by the mid-seventeenth century. An average population is difficult to estimate. However, there must have been at least 500 souls in each. The aggregate for the island might then be 6,500, a number in excess of Mooney's figure (1928: p. 4) of 6,000. The village figure may be approximated by considering the larger, principal villages to have had 300 persons each, and the smaller to have had 150 each. The total would be 7,650

Both these estimates seem too low. The difficulty is, of course, that we do not know the full dimensions of the subtribes prior to white occupation, the complete list of settlements, or the true size of the villages. Southern New York differs from the New England states in that there are recorded no contemporary estimates of size for individual inhabited places. On the basis of the information as it comes to us from Wood, Thompson, Ruttenber, and other nineteenth-century writers, it might be possible to increase Mooney's figure of 6,000 by 20 or 25 percent, but little more. It is therefore desirable and proper to seek some alternative approach to the problem of aboriginal population.

Unlike the Mahican, the Long Island Indians lived and died in their homeland. They did not migrate in large numbers and establish new homes at a distance, or affiliate with other tribes. Hence the decline in population can be observed more or less directly *in situ* in the documents of the seventeenth and eighteenth centuries, as well as in the modern historical accounts. We may assume provisionally a minimum aboriginal population of 6,000 (Mooney, 1928: p. 4).

Krzywicki (1934: p. 418) quotes R. Evelin as saying that in 1648 there were 800 bowmen living on Long Island. This would suggest a population of about 3,000. It is the opinion of Trelease (1960: p. 179) that previously, between 1640 and 1645, the Indians had probably lost 1,000 persons in the civil disturbances of that period. For 1658-1659 Swanton (1952: p. 43) cites an estimate of 500, probably too low for the entire island. This estimate may be confused with that of 500 for the Montauk, mentioned by Hodge (1907: Part I, pp. 934-935). Trelease (1960: p. 179) says that in 1664 the Indian population of the island was under 1,000. He also quotes Denton (1670) as saying that whereas there were six towns in 1644, there were only two small villages in 1670. The location is not stated but is probably on the east end of the island. In 1698 a census showed (Docs. Rel. Col. Hist. New York, Vol. 1, pp. 437-447) that there were 152 Indians in Southampton and 40 Indians in Southold. In 1711 the Assembly (Docs. Rel. Col. Hist. New York, Vol. 5, p. 253) tried to raise 150 Indians on Long Island to serve in the army. Only 50 reported. The numbers taper off until at the time of the American Revolution only 100 or 200 natives were left.

This depletion, which is so obvious regardless of specific figures, must have been in progress since the first appearance of the Europeans, as it was in all parts of the New World which were encountered by the invaders. Three causes are usually assigned: warfare with other Indians and with the whites, diseases introduced by the whites, and social or economic disturbance engendered by the new living conditions.

Warfare was almost continuous on Long Island, although, except for one or two major struggles, it was maintained on a low level. Some of the more conspicuous conflicts were those of the Canarsee with the Mohawk prior to 1630, and the Dutch War of 1640-1645 in which the Canarsee and their allies were slaughtered by the Englishman Underhill and his Dutch confreres (see Cook, 1973b: pp. 9-11). After the middle of the century the Montauk were engaged in a bitter fight with the Narragansett, a struggle in which the Long Islanders on the whole suffered more than did the mainland tribe.

Together with warfare, all writers ascribe the decline in native population to disease, and yet I know of no reference to any specific epidemic before 1658. In that year occurred an outbreak of smallpox which was particularly virulent among the Montauk proper. The mortality ran to "more than half" (Ruttenber, 1872: p. 76) or "nearly two thirds their number" (Prime, 1845: p. 94). The white citizens of Easthampton (Records, 1663, Book 2, p. 91) ordered Indians to stay out of town on pain of whipping "untill they are free of the small poxe. . . ."

Smallpox swept New England in 1633 and certainly must have reached Long Island not long thereafter. Other epidemics undoubtedly were present, but they have not been recorded. At the same time gastrointestinal complaints and respiratory ailments must have been common, and would have become established as endemic disease.

Along with disease went social disintegration which was manifested not only in the collapse of the aboriginal culture but at the same time in the inability to adapt completely to the new civilization. Many symptoms of this process were visible but little of a concrete nature has been put on record by the predominantly white commentators and historians. We can recognize the end result but it is difficult, if not impossible, to document the course of the decline in detail.

A significant contribution to historical demography has been made by H. F. Dobyns (1966). He has shown that over much of the New World the decline in numbers of the native stock reached a level of 4 or 5 percent of the original value. Thereafter the trend began to reverse itself. The lowest point he calls the nadir of population, and if it is known the aboriginal level may be calculated. One simply multiplies the nadir number by 20 or 25. This is perhaps an oversimplified formula, but it gives a correct answer in several cases. On Long Island, and in New England and the Northeast generally, the method encounters an obstacle because there is no nadir value, after the attainment of which the population increases. In most instances the decline merely continues until the operative group disappears totally, by outright extinction, by absorption into other tribal entities, or by miscegenation and the development of a hybrid race. Dobyns recognizes this difficulty and suggests that in such cases the base (or nadir) number be taken as the population 130 years after contact. This value is appropriate to Mexico, California, and other parts of Latin America, but for eastern North America the period is too long and should be shortened to roughly 100 years. The multiplicative factor of 20 or 25 may also be somewhat too great in some instances, and it may be wise to consider reducing it to 15 or even less as other circumstances dictate. In general terms, however, the Dobyns principle appears to hold.

## CONCLUSION

For Long Island the figures given previously indicate a very small population one hundred years after first contact. For practical purposes this event may be taken as ca. 1610, with the arrival of the Dutch, although the Long Island people had encountered explorers and fishermen for decades before this date. In 1698 there were 192 Indians in two towns at the eastern end of the island. In several other censuses, taken at about the same time, there is no record of any Indians. In 1711, when the Assembly tried to raise 150 men among them, the legislators must have thought that there were at least 600 people surviving. But only 50 responded, a turn-out which represents a population of only 200. The idea that the other 100 were hiding is not necessarily true; they may not have been in existence. If there were less than 1,000, as Trelease (1960: p. 179) thinks, after 1664, the remainder fifty years later must have been no more than a very few hundred. However, Thompson (1839: p. 65) says that in 1761 the Montauk had 38 families, and Swanton (1952: p. 43) puts the number in 1788 at 162. A fair compromise among these scattered estimates is an Indian population of 300 in 1710. If we now apply Dobyns' factor of 25 we get an aboriginal population of 7,500 on Long Island.

Still another approach is by means of a density calculation. It was found that the density of the Nauset on Cape Cod was 5.5 persons per square mile, whereas that of more inland tribes was lower, and that of the Indians on the larger offshore islands was much higher. The terrain and environment of Long Island resembles most closely that of Cape Cod, although the northern coast of the island is more protected and more replete with food resources than the Cape. On the basis of the similarity a density of 6.0 for Long Island may be assumed. The area by planimeter measurement is 1,310 square miles, but many of the smaller islands had to be omitted from the calculation. The total area may be taken as 1,400 square miles. With a density of 6.0 persons per square mile, the total population would have been 8,400 souls.

There are now four estimates: subtribal counts, village counts, Dobyns' depletion factor, and density. The respective estimates for total population are 6,500, 7,650, 7,500, and 8,400. These are all reasonably close together. The average, which will be accepted, is approximately 7,500.

## SUMMARY

By the use of various methods a probable aboriginal population has been estimated for the tribes of New England and southeastern New York in 1610. The values presented in the body of this essay are as follows:

| | | | |
|---|---|---|---|
| Pennacook | 12,000 | Nipmuck - Connecticut Valley | 5,300 |
| Massachusetts | 4,500 | Wappinger Confederacy | 13,200 |
| Wampanoag | 5,000 | Mahican | 5,000 |
| Nauset and the islands | 8,100 | Long Island | 7,500 |
| Narragansett | 7,800 | | |
| Mohegan - Pequot | 3,500 | Total | 71,900 |

Although there is the appearance of precision, complete accuracy cannot be claimed. The total is given as approximately 72,000, but a range from 60,000 to 80,000 must be understood. Furthermore, if the Indian population of this region was truly given by the counts of the late eighteenth century, and if the magnitude of the decline even approximated that proposed by Dobyns and other recent scholars, the estimate made here is far too low. Nevertheless, the historical and in part the archaeological evidence does not warrant a profound increase in the estimated population.

# BIBLIOGRAPHY

ANONYMOUS
  1802   *A Description and History of Eastham, in the County of Barnstable. In:* Mass. Hist. Soc., Coll., Series 1, Vol. 8, pp. 154-186.
ANONYMOUS
  1807   *A Description of Duke's County. In:* Mass. Hist. Soc., Coll., Series 2, Vol. 3, pp. 38-94 (Published in 1815).
ANONYMOUS
  1809   *Memoir of the Pequots. In:* Mass. Hist. Soc., Coll., Series 1, Vol. 10, pp. 101-105.
ANONYMOUS
  n.d.   *Indians on Connecticut River. In:* Stiles Documents, Mass. Hist. Soc., Coll., Series 1, Vol. 5, pp. 112-113.
BALLARD, REV. EDWARD
  1866   *Character of the Pennacooks. In:* New Hampshire Hist. Soc., Coll., Vol. 8, pp. 428-445.
BARSTOW, GEORGE
  1842   *The History of New Hampshire.* Concord, New Hampshire.
BENNETT, M. K.
  1955   *The Food Economy of the New England Indians, 1605-1675.* Journal of Political Economy, Vol. 63, pp. 369-397.
BIRDSEY, REV. NATHAN
  1761   *Letter to Rev. E. Stiles. In:* Mass. Hist. Soc., Coll., Series 1, Vol. 10, pp. 111-112.
BOLTON, ROBERT
  1881   *The History of Several Towns, Manors, and Patents of the County of Westchester . . . .* 2 vols., Ed. by Rev. C. W. Bolton. New York: Charles F. Roper.
BOURNE, RICHARD
  1674   See Gookin.
BRACKENRIDGE, H. M.
  1814   *Views of Lousiana Together with a Journal of a Voyage up the Missouri River in 1811.* Pittsburgh. Cited by L. Krzywicki (1934), p. 318.
BRADFORD, WILLIAM
  1620-  *History of Plymouth Plantation.* Edition of Massachusetts Legislature, 1897. Boston:
  1647   Wright and Potter Printing Co., 1901.
BROWN, PERCY S.
  1952   *The Indian Fort at Lochmere, New Hampshire.* New Hampshire Archaeologist, No. 3, pp. 1-8.
BULLEN, RIPLEY P.
  1941   *Report of the Site Survey to February, 1941.* Mass. Archaeol. Soc., Bull., Vol. 2, No. 3, pp. 2-9.
  1949   *Excavations in Northeastern Massachusetts.* Peabody Foundation for Archaeology, Papers, Vol. 1, No. 3, pp. 1-152.
BUSHNELL, DAVID I., JR.
  1919   *Native Villages and Village Sites East of the Mississippi.* Bureau of American Ethnology, Bull., No. 69, pp. 1-111.
BUTLER, EVA L.
  1948   *Algonkian Culture and Use of Maize in Southern New England.* Archaeol. Soc. of Connecticut, Bull. No. 22, pp. 3-39.
CALLENDAR, JOHN
  1739   *An Historical Discourse . . . [on] the Colony of Rhode Island. In:* Rhode Island Hist. Soc., Coll., Vol. 4. Published in 1838.

CHAMPLAIN, SAMUEL DE
  1604-      *Voyages of Samuel de Champlain,* ed. by W. L. Grant. Original Narratives of Early
  1618       American History, J. Franklin Jameson, gen. ed. New York: Scribner's, 1907.
COOK, SHERBURNE F.
  1973a      *The Significance of Disease in the Extinction of the New England Indians.* Human
             Biology, Vol. 45, pp. 485-508.
  1973b      *Interracial Warfare and Population Decline Among the New England Indians.* Ethno-
             history, Vol. 20, pp. 1-24.
COOK, SHERBURNE F., and ROBERT F. HEIZER
  1968       *Relationship Among Houses, Settlement Areas, and Population in Aboriginal
             California.* Chap. VI *in:* Settlement Archaeology, ed. by K. C. Chang. Palo Alto,
             Calif.: National Press Books.
DAY, GORDON M.
  1962       *English-Indian Contacts in New England.* Ethnohistory, Vol. 9, pp. 24-40.
DAY, GORDON M.
  1965       *The Identity of the Sokokis.* Ethnohistory, Vol. 12, pp. 237-249.
DE FOREST, JOHN W.
  1853       *History of the Indians of Connecticut from the Earliest Known Period to 1850.*
             Hartford, Conn.: W. J. Hamersley.
DELABARRE, EDWARD B., and HARRIS H. WILDER
  1920       *Indian Corn Hills in Massachusetts.* American Anthropologist, Vol. 22, pp. 203-225.
DEVOTION, REV. JOHN
  1761       *Letter to Rev. Dr. Gates. In:* Mass. Hist. Soc., Coll., Series 1, Vol. 10, pp. 105-111.
DOBYNS, HENRY F.
  1966       *An Appraisal of Techniques with a New Hemispheric Estimate.* Current Anthropology,
             Vol. 7, pp. 395-416.
DOCUMENTS RELATIVE TO THE COLONIAL HISTORY OF THE STATE OF NEW YORK.
  1853-      15 vols., various eds. Albany, N.Y.: Weed, Parsons and Co.
  1887
DORR, HENRY C.
  1885       *The Narragansetts. In:* Rhode Island Hist. Soc. Coll., Vol. 7, pp. 135-237.
DOUGLAS, W.
  1760       *A Summary, Historical and Political, of the First Planting . . . of the British Settle-
             ments in North America.* London. See esp. Vol. 1, p. 192.
DRAKE, SAMUEL G.
  1851       *Biography and History of the Indians of North America, from its First Discovery.*
             11th edition. Boston: B. B. Mussey.
  1867       *The Old Indian Chronicle.* Introduction: Origin of Indian Wars, pp. 1-118. Boston:
             Samuel A. Drake.
DUDLEY, GOV. THOMAS
  1631       *Letter to the Countess of Lincoln. In:* Force (1838), Vol. 2, No. 4.
ELLIS, GEORGE W., and JOHN E. MORRIS
  1906       *King Philip's War.* New York: Grafton Press.
FARMER, JOHN
  1824       *Note on the Pennacook Indians in New Hampshire. In:* New Hampshire Hist. Soc.,
             Coll., Vol. 1, pp. 218-227 Concord, N. H.
FORCE, PETER
  1838       *Tracts and Other Papers, Relating Principally to the Origin, Settlement, and Progress
             of the Colonies of North America.* Vol. 2. Washington, D. C. (Contains several papers,
             listed here under the names of the authors.)
GAHAN, LAWRENCE K.
  1941       *The Nipmucks and Their Territory.* Mass. Archaeol. Soc., Bull., Vol. 2, No. 4, pp. 2-6.

GOOKIN, DANIEL
1674    *Historical Collections of the Indians in New England. In:* Mass. Hist. Soc., Coll.,
        Series 1, Vol. 1, pp. 141-232. Originally published in 1792, and reprinted in 1806.
HADLEY, AMOS
1903    *Aboriginal Occupation. In: History of Concord, N. H.,* ed. by James O. Lyford, Chap.
        1, pp. 65-94. Published by City History Commission, Concord, N. H. Concord: Rum-
        ford Press.
HARE, LLOYD C. M.
1932    *Thomas Mayhew, Patriarch to the Indians.* New York: D. Appleton
HAWLEY, --
1698    *see* Rawson, Grindal, and Samuel Danforth.
HIGGESON, --
1629    *New England's Plantation. In:* Mass. Hist. Soc., Coll., Series 1, Vol. 1, pp. 117-125.
        Published in 1792.
HINCKLEY, GOV. THOMAS
1685    *Letter to William Stoughton and Joseph Dudley. In:* Mass. Hist. Soc., Coll.,
        Series 4, Vol. 5, pp. 132-134. Published in 1861.
HODGE, FREDERICK W., ed.
1907,   *Handbook of American Indians North of Mexico.* Bureau of American Ethnology,
1910    Bull., No. 30. 2 parts: Part I, 1907; Part II, 1910. Washington, D. C.: Smithsonian
        Institution.
HOLMES, ABIEL
1804    *Memoir of the Mohegans. In:* Mass. Hist. Soc., Coll., Series 1, Vol. 9, pp. 75-99.
HOYT, EPAPHRAS
1824    *Antiquarian Researches: A History of the Indian Wars in the Country Bordering
        the Connecticut River.* Greenfield, Mass.
HUBBARD, WILLIAM
1680    *A General History of New England. In:* Mass. Hist. Soc., Coll., Series 2, Vols. 5 and
        6, pp. 1-676. Published in 1815.
HUDEN, JOHN C.
1960    *see* Ritchie, William A.
1962    *Indian Groups in Vermont.* New Hampshire Archaeologist, No. 11, pp. 8-10.
JAMESON, JOHN F., ed.
1909    *Narratives of New Netherland,* 1609-1664. New York: Scribner's.
JOHNSON, EDWARD
1654    *Wonder-Working Providence of Sion's Savior in New England. In:* Mass. Hist. Soc.,
        Coll., Series 2, Vol. 2, pp. 49-96. Published in 1819.
JOSSELYN, JOHN
1673    *An Account of Two Voyages to New England. In:* Mass. Hist. Soc., Coll., Series 3,
        Vol. 3, pp. 211-354. Published in 1833.
JUDD, SYLVESTER
1905    *History of Hadley.* Springfield, Mass.
KIDDER, FREDERICK
1859    *The Abenaki Indians. In:* Coll. Maine Hist. Soc., Vol. 6, pp. 229-263.
KRZYWICKI, LUDWIK
1934    *Primitive Society and Its Vital Statistics.* London: MacMillan and Co.
             Appendix II. North American Indian Tribes, pp. 318-509.
             Appendix III. North American Confederacies and Their Equivalents, pp. 510-543.
LAET, JOHAN DE
1625    *New World, or Description of West-India.* Book III, Chap. 7, *in: Narratives of New
        Netherland, 1609-1664,* ed. by J. Franklin Jameson, pp. 29-60. New York: Scribner's,
        1909.

LAURENT, STEPHEN
  1959    *The Diet That Made the Red Man.* New Hampshire Archaeologist, No. 9, pp. 6-9.
LESCARBOT, MARC
  1612    *L'Histoire de la Nouvelle France.* Transl. by W. L. Grant and H. P. Biggar as *The History of New France.* Published by Champlain Society, Vol. 7. Toronto, 1907-1914.
MC CLURE, DAVID
  1797    Letter: *Settlement and Antiquities of the Town of Windsor in Connecticut.* Stiles Documents, Mass. Hist. Soc., Coll., Series 1, Vol. 5, pp. 166-171.
MACY, ZACCHEUS
  1792    *A Short Journal of the First Settlement of the Island of Nantucket . . . . In:* Mass. Hist. Soc., Coll., Series 1, Vol. 3, pp. 155-160. Published in 1910.
MARSHALL, HARLAN A.
  1942    *Some Ancient Indian Village Sites Adjacent to Manchester, New Hampshire.* American Antiquity, Vol. 7, pp. 359-363.
MOONEY, JAMES
  1907    *Mohegan. In: Handbook of American Indians North of Mexico,* ed. Frederick W. Hodge. Bureau of American Ethnology, Bull., No. 30, Part I, pp. 926-927.
  1910a   *Narragansett. In: Handbook,* Part II, pp. 28-30.
  1910b   *Pequot. In: Handbook,* Part II, pp. 229-231.
  1928    *The Aboriginal Population of America North of Mexico.* Smithsonian Misc. Coll., Vol. 80, No. 7, pp. 1-40.
MOONEY, JAMES, and CYRUS THOMAS
  1910    *Pennacook. In: Handbook of American Indians North of Mexico,* ed. Frederick W. Hodge. Bureau of American Ethnology, Bull., No. 30, Part II, pp. 225-226.
MOOREHEAD, WARREN K.
  1931    *The Merrimack Archaeological Survey: A Preliminary Paper.* Published by Peabody Museum, Salem, Mass., pp. 1-79.
MORSE, J.
  1822    *A Report to the Secretary of War of the United States, on Indian Affairs . . . .* New Haven: S. Converse.
MORTON, THOMAS
  1632    *New English Canaan. In:* Force (1838): Vol. 2, No. 5.
MOURT, --
  1622    *Relation or Journal of a Plantation Settled at Plymouth in New England, and Proceedings Thereof.* Abridged in *Purchas's Pilgrims,* London, 1625, Book 10, Chap. 4. Reprinted in Mass. Hist., Soc., Coll., Series 1, Vol. 8, pp. 203-239, 1802.
ORR, CHARLES
  1897    *History of the Pequot War.* Reprints of Mason, Underhill, Vincent, Gardiner; all from Mass. Hist. Soc., Coll. Continuous paging. Cleveland, Ohio: Helman Taylor Co.
PERKINS, G. H.
  1909    *Aboriginal Remains in the Champlain Valley.* American Anthropologist, N.S., Vol. 11, pp. 607-623.
PHELPS, MASON
  1948    *Indians of Old Brookfield.* Excerpts from *History of North Brookfield* by Josiah H. Temple, 1887. Mass. Archaeol. Soc., Bull., Vol. 9, No. 4, pp. 80-82. No citations of original page numbers.
POTTER, C. E.
  1865    *Pennacooks. In: Archives of Aboriginal Knowledge . . . ,* 6 vols., ed. Henry R. Schoolcraft, Vol. 5, pp. 217-237. Philadelphia: J. B. Lippincott.
POTTER, ELISHA R., JR.
  1835    *The Early History of the Narragansett Country. In:* Rhode Island Hist. Soc., Coll., Vol. 3, pp. 1-315.

PRICE, CHESTER B.
1967    *Historic Indian Trails of New Hampshire.* New Hampshire Archaeologist, No. 14, pp. 1-12.

PRIME, NATHANIEL S.
1845    *A History of Long Island.* New York: Robert Carter.

QUANAPAUG, JAMES
1675    *James Quanapaug's Information. In:* Mass. Hist. Soc., Coll., Series 1, Vol. 6, pp. 205-208. Published in 1800.

RASIERES, ISAACK DE
1628    *Letter to Samuel Blommaert. In: Narratives of New Netherland, 1609-1664,* ed. by J. Franklin Jameson, pp. 97-115. New York: Scribner's, 1909.

RAWSON, REV. MR. GRINDAL, and REV. MR. SAMUEL DANFORTH
1698    *Account of an Indian Visitation, A.D. 1698 . . . .* Stiles Documents, Mass. Hist. Soc., Coll., Series 1, Vol. 10, pp. 129-134.

RITCHIE, WILLIAM A.
1961    Review of: *Archaeology in Vermont, Supplemented by Materials from New England and New York,* by John C. Huden, 1960. University of Vermont, Monograph No. 3, 107 pp., Burlington, Vt.

RUTTENBER, EDWARD M.
1872    *History of the Indian Tribes of Hudson's River.* Albany, N. Y.: J. Munsell.

SHERMAN, THEODORE H.
1941    *A Cave Habitation in Vermont.* American Antiquity, Vol. 7, pp. 176-178.

SMITH, CAPTAIN JOHN
1616    *A Description of New England . . . . In:* Mass. Hist. Soc., Coll., Series 3, Vol. 6, pp. 95-140, 1837; also *in:* Force's *Tracts,* Vol. 2, No. 1, pp. 1-48, 1838.
1622    *New England's Trials. In:* Force's *Tracts,* Vol. 2, No. 2, pp. 1-24, 1838.
1631    *Advertisements for the Inexperienced Planters of New England, or anywhere . . . . In:* Mass. Hist. Soc., Coll., Series 3, Vol. 3, pp. 1-53. Published in 1833.

SPECK, FRANK G.
1928a   *Native Tribes and Dialects of Connecticut; A Mohegan-Pequot Diary.* Bureau of American Ethnology, Annual Report, No. 43, pp. 199-287.
1928b   *Territorial Subdivisions and Boundaries of the Wampanoag, Massachusetts, and Nauset Indians.* Museum of the American Indian, Heye Foundation, Misc. Series, No. 44, pp. 1-152.

SPIESS, MATHIAS
1937    *Podunk Indian Sites.* Archaeol. Soc. of Connecticut, Bull., No. 5, pp. 9-11. Reprinted in 1962.

STILES DOCUMENTS
1792    *An Account of the Potenummecut Indians. Taken by Dr. Stiles . . . , June 4, 1792.* Mass. Hist. Soc., Coll., Series 1, Vol. 10, p. 113. (Other Stiles Documents are listed here under the names of the individual authors.)

STRACHEY, WILLIAM
1612    *The Historie of Travaile into Virginia. The Second Book. In:* Mass. Hist. Soc., Coll., Series 4, Vol. 1, pp. 219-246, 1852. (Originally published in 1612.)

SWANTON, JOHN R.
1952    *The Indian Tribes of North America. In:* Bureau of American Ethnology, Bull., No. 145.

SYLVESTER, HERBERT M.
1910    *Indian Wars of New England.* 3 vols. Boston: W. B. Clarke.

THOMPSON, BENJAMIN F.
1839    *History of Long Island.* New York.

THORNTON, J. WINGATE
 1857 *Ancient Pemaquid: An Historical Review. In:* Maine Hist. Soc., Coll., Vol. 5, pp. 139-305.

TOWNSHEND, CHARLES H.
 1900 *A Pictorial History of "Raynham" and Its Vicinity.* New Haven: Tuttle, Morehouse and Taylor.

TRELEASE, ALLEN W.
 1960 *Indian Affairs in Colonial New York: The Seventeenth Century.* Ithaca, N. Y.: Cornell University Press.

TRUMBULL, BENJAMIN
 1767 *A Compendium of the Indian Wars in New England . . . ,* ed. by Frederick B. Hartrauft. Hartford, Conn., 1926.

UNDERHILL, JOHN
 1638 *Newes from America; or a New and Experimentall Discoverie of New England. In:* Mass. Hist. Soc., Coll., Series 3, Vol. 6, pp. 1-28. Published in 1837. (See also, Orr, 1897.)

VAUGHAN, ALDEN T.
 1965 *New England Frontier: Puritans and Indians, 1620-1675.* Boston and Toronto: Little, Brown.

VINCENT, P.
 1638 *A True Relation of the Late Battell Fought in New England Between the English and the Pequot Savages. In:* Mass. Hist. Soc., Coll., Series 3, Vol. 6, pp. 29-44. Published in 1837. (See also Orr, 1897.)

WHITE, JOHN
 1630 *The Planters Plea. In:* Force (1838), Vol. 2, No. 3.

WILLARD, JOSEPH
 1826 *History of Lancaster. In:* Worcester Magazine and Historical Journal, Vol. 2, pp. 257-323.

WILLIAMS, ROGER
 1637-38 *Letters to John Winthrop. In:* Mass. Hist. Soc., Coll., Series 4, Vol. 6, pp. 184-311.
 1643 *A Key into the Language of America; or an Help to the Language of the Natives in . . . New England.* London. Reprinted in Rhode Island Hist. Soc., Coll., Vol. 1, 1827.
 1676 *Letter to Gov. John Leveret of Massachusetts Colony,* dated 16 August, 1676. *In:* Mass. Hist. Soc., Coll., Series 3, Vol. 1, pp. 70-72, 1825.

WILLIAMSON, WILLIAM D.
 1839 *The History of the State of Maine.* 2 vols. Hallowell, Maine.

WILLOUGHBY, CHARLES C.
 1935 *Antiquities of the New England Indians.* 314 pp. Published by Peabody Museum, Harvard Unitversity, Cambridge, Mass.

WINSLOW, EDWARD
 1625 *Good News from New England; or a Relation of Things Remarkable in that Plantation. In:* Mass. Hist. Soc., Coll., Series 1, Vol. 8, pp. 239-276. Published in 1802.

WINTHROP, JOHN
 1630-49 *Winthrop's Journal, "History of New England," 1630-1649. In: Original Narratives of Early American History,* ed. by J. Franklin Jameson. New York: Barnes and Noble, 1908.

WINTHROP, JOHN JR.
 1664 *Letter to Roger Williams,* dated 6 February, 1664. *In:* Mass. Hist. Soc., Coll., Series 4, Vol. 6, p. 531.

WOOD, SILAS
 1828 *A Sketch of the First Settlement of the Several Towns on Long Island . . . .,* new edition. Brooklyn: Alden Spooner.

WOOD, WILLIAM
  1634   *New England's Prospect.* London. Printed for the Prince Society, Boston, 1865, Vol. III. Reprinted in Research and Source Works Series, No. 131. New York: Burt Franklin, 1967.

WRIGHT, HARRY A.
  1949   *The Story of Western Massachusetts,* Vol. 1. New York: Lewis Historical Publishing Co.

088109